GOLF AND MARRIAGE

IMPROVE YOUR MARRIAGE
BY IMPROVING YOUR GOLF

BY

DR. GAREY A. JOHNSON

To

Adrian, Paloma, and Marie-Jeanne

and a special dedication to my late uncle
Mr. John 'Jake' Robinson
who once told me,
"Boy, you need to learn golf!"

Golf and marriage are two of the hardest things a person attempts in a lifetime, because in both your biggest enemy is yourself. Golf can routinely make you want to walk away and never come back, and who hasn't experienced that same feeling about their marriage? At the core, both golf and marriage are about learning to observe and understand your emotions and directing them for a happy outcome. The good news is, the same techniques that can do this for your golf game can also do it for your marriage.

—Garey A. Johnson

Table of Contents

Introduction

Golf is a billion-dollar industry devoted entirely to hope.
—Deepak Chopra

I never knew what real happiness was until I got married.
And by then it was too late.
—Max Kauffmann

Why is golf so hard? Simply put, there are a multitude of factors—some very subtle—that conspire to dictate the outcome of your efforts.

Why is marriage so hard? Simply put, there are a multitude of factors—some very subtle—that conspire to dictate the outcome of your efforts.

The Rev (a true story)

The starter told me to proceed to the number one tee, as the gentleman I'd be playing with was already there. It was a beautiful fall day in the southern part of the San Francisco Bay Area, and I was very much looking forward to an enjoyable practice round.

He introduced himself as Bob. I learned later he was Reverend Bob—a genteel, soft-spoken man of the cloth, whose age I would guess to be in the mid-fifties. He told me he preached at a church somewhere in nearby San Jose, and also that he was a three handicap.

After the first few holes I was totally convinced about his being a three. His first drive soared high and drew along the confines of the 385-yard par four, splitting the fairway and coming to rest about a three-quarter nine iron from center green. His approach (he hit pitching wedge) landed softly, then released to within about eight feet of the pin. Meanwhile, I managed to come out of the rough in pretty good shape and was putting for par from about five feet. He made birdie and congratulated me on my scramble save.

The second hole was a straight-on par four, only 370 yards but very narrow, with the landing area made even narrower by an expansive bunker gobbling up the right third of the fairway. Reverend Bob pulled out a hybrid and blistered a low stinger-like shot that landed just left of the bunker and raced an additional fifty yards or so, setting him up for another short-iron approach. He missed birdie as his double-breaking putt just lipped out. Me? I had to settle for the dreaded three-putt bogey.

So this is how it went for pretty much all of the front nine. At the turn he was even par and I was four over. He was very calm, friendly and talkative in a way you might expect a minister to be. We discussed politics, local economics, religion, and of course—golf.

At number fifteen, a sharp dogleg par five with lots of trouble, he launched a beautiful power fade that caught the corner just right, setting him up to make a comfortable go for the green on his second shot. As we walked down the fairway (yep, I kept it on the short grass this time) I brought up the subject of marriage and family. I told him I had been married five years and so far so good. He indicated he was in his twenty-fourth year of marriage, had three children ranging in age from sixteen to twenty-two, and then mumbled something about his wife that I couldn't quite understand but realized, from his body language, that it would probably be a good idea to change the subject.

He sliced his next shot something fierce. It didn't go out of bounds but was right on the edge in deep rough, and while I couldn't be sure, I believe I heard him launch an expletive towards his ball which sounded like it invoked his Master. Meanwhile, I managed a reasonably controlled fairway metal to a point well inside the hundred-yard marker and was set to try to get my third shot within birdie range. Reverend Bob's woes continued. He chopped it out of the rough only to get a "fried egg" in the backside face of a greenside bunker—another expletive. Two shots later he was on the edge of the green and three-putted for triple bogey.

So he got triple bogey on fifteen, he bogeyed sixteen, had to scramble for par on seventeen (a short par-three) and bogeyed eighteen. I thought to myself, *What just happened?* Since we had briefly brought up marriage back on the fifteenth fairway, he had been completely taken out of his game and was, basically, in terms of his golf swing, an entirely different person.

We shook hands, he thanked me for the round and apologized for his play on the last four holes, then he turned and walked away. I never saw him again. End of story.

Was Reverend Bob really apologizing because he hit a few bad shots (I hit a bunch of them), or was he apologizing because his attitude soured when he started talking about his wife? Maybe I owed him an apology for even bringing up the subject of marriage and family back on number fifteen.

It made me think about other incidences over the years when one of the guys in my foursome would make it known he was on the golf course that day because he needed to get away from what was going on at home. Often, it seemed, these same guys would be experiencing their golf in ways similar to what they were lamenting about how their home life was going. They would be agonizing over real and very intense frustration; there would be exclamations about lack of control or lack of understanding; the "why am I here" type questions would seem genuinely baffling and serious. For sure, if the "old lady" was mentioned at all, it would accompany complaints and exhortations that only came after bad shots, a particularly bad hole, or maybe eighteen bad holes. I've never heard anyone mention his wife after making birdie.

This was a familiar refrain, whether it was a golf course on the East Coast, on the West Coast, at a five-star resort, or the local municipal track.

This made me think there must be some universal truths about the similarities in how golf and marriage tend to work on the average person. The more I thought about it, the more it made sense that both golf and marriage force one to deal with oneself and come up against the characteristics of his or her personality in ways that are similar. Golf isn't marriage, and marriage isn't golf, but they both give you the opportunity to choose where you'd like to experience today's most intense frustrations.

Doctor Joseph Parent, PGA coach and Buddhist teacher, wrote a book about mastering golf's mental game. In it, he wrote, "When putting, expand your mind beyond the cup ... see the whole green."

If you can do that for your marriage—that is, recognize all the bigger factors that led up to your spouse's saying or doing what he or she said or did—you'll see those marriage "putts" going in more often, too.

Figure A

Figure A should be familiar to all golfers. The multitude of factors that can affect what happens after you start your swing may, at times, seem as much mystical as physical. Anything, from how the ball sits on the ground to how tight your underwear happens to be that morning, can influence the outcome of your attempt to advance the ball toward the hole. The frustration grows for most golfers as they focus more and more on the mechanics of their swing, the type of equipment they are using, the layout of the course, and other extraneous things.

Of course you need to learn the swing basics, but that only gets you part of the way there. Eventually you have to figure out how to shrink that little thought bubble above your head to a point where pretty much all those thoughts go away. At that point, your golf swing becomes more of a subconscious action, and you get closer to what some teaching professionals like to refer to as "automatic golf." An effortless ease awaits any golfer who can learn to do this. Your golf swing is an expression of who you are—at this moment. It reflects your moods, quirks in your personality, and, ultimately, where you are in your evolution as a human being.

Figure B

The scene in Figure B? No explanation needed. We've all been there. That thought bubble is just as much a distraction as the one in Figure A and can be the start of a very long day--or night.

It's important not to take oneself too seriously when trying to understand the differences between men and women. Learning to laugh when forced to face the frustrations of marriage (and golf) is a good thing. We should all learn to have fun with it and laugh more--just for the health of it.

The Genie

This guy found a peculiar-looking bottle and rubbed it to clean it off.
A genie emerged and told him to make a wish.
The guy said, "I love going to Hawaii but can't afford the plane fare. Can you build me a bridge so I can drive to Hawaii?"
The genie said, "Sorry, but that's impossibly difficult and would be too dangerous. Is there something else I can do for you?"
The guy said, "Okay, can you tell me the secret to understanding women?"
The genie said, "Did you want one or two lanes on that bridge?"

It was suggested to me that, instead of *Golf and Marriage*, a better title for this book would be *Golf or Marriage*. I understand the point. The Holy Bible says something about not being able to serve two masters. For many married golfers, it often feels like you're desperately trying to do exactly that. You only have so much time and energy available each day. Your golf and your marriage each seem to demand it all!

Chapter 1

Bad Marriages and Bad Golf Hurt Each Other

My husband and I have never considered divorce...
murder sometimes, but never divorce.
—Joyce Brothers

You can make a lot of money in this game [golf].
Just ask my ex-wives.

Both of them are so rich that neither of their husbands work.
—Lee Trevino

Men are from Mars, women are from Venus.

Bad golf and bad marriages are from the Twilight Zone.

In golf there is something called the *slope rating*, which is expressed as a number usually between 110 and 150. The slope rating is a relative measure of how hard a golf course is based on its architecture, which includes such things as length, narrowness of fairways, size of the greens, and placement, number, and types of hazards, and so forth. Generally speaking, the higher the slope rating, the tougher the golf course.

In marriage, there is something I would call the *dope rating*. The dope rating speaks to how aware you are and how prepared you are to deal with what you're getting into when you say "I do." The higher dope ratings come in various situations: where one or both of you expect marriage to be just a continuation of the dating life, or a case of "love at first sight," or after a particularly great party in Las Vegas or Cabo! Also, generally speaking, the younger you are when you decide to get married, the higher your dope rating will be.

In marriage, as in golf, looks and early impressions can be very deceiving. If you're not careful before you make that big decision to move forward, you might eventually wind up asking yourself, *why the hell am I here dealing with this?*

I've heard it said that women marry in hopes they can change the man, while a man marries hoping the woman doesn't change, so from that perspective I guess we could also characterize a marriage by something called the *hope rating*.

Marriage and golf both force you into an ongoing effort to figure out how to increase your P/S (pleasure-to-strife) ratio.

In golf you might be thinking you need to beat the other players or beat the course or beat the weather. Eventually, you come to realize it's not about beating any of those things. What it is about is *not* beating yourself. By this I mean you have to try to figure out what's going on with that person who's swinging the golf club.

Or here's another way to think of it. You need to learn to release your inner Bagger Vance, that guru we all have somewhere deep inside who's usually crusted over with various forms of emotional "ground under repair." In marriage, it sometimes feels like there's so much going on that no matter how hard you try to release the guru, you just can't seem to get unstuck.

Much of this is related to the basic differences in the natures of men and women. For example, most women like to express what they're feeling and are therefore inclined to let you know about it immediately. Most men, on the other hand, tend not to show a reaction to what they're feeling until it becomes so intense that the reaction becomes more like an explosion. This is when dogs get kicked and golf clubs go flying.

The average person is bound to feel beaten about the head and shoulders in his golf and his marriage from time to time. He typically deals with this by toughing it out, showing strength and resolve, and finding a sanctuary. Golf can be a good sanctuary from marriage, but marriage isn't much good as a sanctuary from golf.

Most of those who eventually quit golf say things like, *This is just crazy, It takes too much time, It's too expensive, It has too many rules, and It's so hard I just can't get it down.* In marriage the reasons given for getting out are often the same—too expensive, too many rules, too much time, and so hard you just can't get it down.

I've been asked how you can compare something like golf, which is just a game, to marriage, which is such a serious thing. I'm not comparing the importance of golf to that of marriage, I'm pointing out the parallels that exist between the two in the ways they tend to challenge the average human being mentally and emotionally. Marriage and golf can both take a person from feeling like a world-beater to feeling like a world-beggar in the blink of an eye. The difference between the two feelings has mainly to do with who you think you are and why you are where you are.

Why golf?

If you want a linguistic adventure,
go drinking with a Scotsman…
and how they could invent a sport like golf!
—Robin Williams

Here's one idea (mine) about why golf was invented: Those Scots of old were in search of a surrogate for their marriages—some kind of activity that would give them practice in dealing with the challenges at home. They wanted a way to simulate the same intense feelings and be able to practice managing their reactions when faced with inexplicable phenomena. These guys were in search of a way to be tested—in a less consequential space—so when they got home they could generate more happiness there.

There are ten key questions a person will eventually ask himself or herself about both golf and marriage:

1. Why have I subjected myself to this?

2. Will I live long enough and have the time and energy to learn to do this well?

3. How in the hell do you actually become good at this?

4. How am I doing? I know I'm a talented person no matter how it looks.

5. In what ways do I have to change to be successful at this?

6. Who can I talk to for help?

7. Is doing this worth putting up with all the frustration?

8. Is there an easier way to have success at this?

9. What's the best way to just walk away?

10. What's the downside if I decide to quit?

Finding answers to those questions is a big part of this adventure we call life. Answering them for your golf game will help you gain some insight on answering them for your marriage.

Golf is an ultimate head game, in that every time you tee it up, you know there's trouble waiting for you on every hole. How you prepare yourself, not only to deal with the trouble, but also with how you'll feel about having to deal with it, will largely dictate what you get out of that round. It's the same for marriage. The hazards are many, and you know they're out in front of you for as long as you stay in the marriage. Here's the big question: How will you relate to them and eventually figure out how to make them work for you and your spouse?

At times both your marriage and your golf swing can be pure, simple, peaceful, and agreeable and bring you years of great pleasure. At other times they both can be mean, unstable, violent, and confusing and bring you years of glorious frustration.

For most of us, our marriage, like our golf swing, will be agreeable one day and highly frustrating the next. Or it may be quite peaceful one minute and a complete conundrum a minute or two later. The roller coaster ride that is marriage happens for exactly the same reason it does with your golf game. If you learn to ride the golf roller coaster well, you can get much better at riding the marriage roller coaster.

Buddhist doctrine teaches that if you're in a "disagreeable marriage" you must say bye-bye to enlightenment. Golf can do that to you as well. Bad golf, like a bad marriage, will happen if you're constantly searching for outside answers to inside issues. Searching within yourself will help you resolve one of the key causes of bad golf and bad marriages, the essence of which is a lack of understanding about what you were trying to do when you decided to do it in the first place.

Bad marriages happen when two people can't seem to understand each other. Bad golf happens when one person can't seem to understand himself or herself.

Some people put almost all of their focus on the mechanics of the golf swing. If you only address swing mechanics, it's like trying to get your wife to agree with you because you believe you're able to explain to her the logic of the situation. Good luck with that! Like bad golf, bad marriages will reflect aspects of your character that are the result of a lifetime of nature-and-nurture influences, so you need to be willing to peel back a few layers if you want to figure out what's going on.

Some relationship researchers believe finding the ideal partner for marriage will always amount to a coin toss, because you need someone with complementary levels of such hormones as dopamine, serotonin, testosterone, and estrogen for the relationship to work well. It would be great if scientists could come up with a way to know immediately, upon meeting someone, what levels of those hormones are present and how they compare to your own. There should be an app for that!

Bad golf and bad marriages happen when you have expectations that are unrealistic, or when you fail to understand the nature of the environment you're subjecting yourself to. You might find a partner who'll treat you like a king or queen for a while but you'll never find a golf swing that will ever treat you any better than you treat yourself.

In marriage you're constantly trying to get your partner to understand how you want to be treated. You expect your spouse to understand, and then do, the things that make you feel good. But in order to get what you want at home, you'll need to show him or her that you know, yourself, what it takes to make you feel good.

Likewise, your golf swing will demand that you know how to make yourself feel good before it will give you what you want on the golf course.

Are you committed to the idea that the only way you and your spouse will ever split up is when one of you dies? If that's not a goal for you, then what are you fully committed to for your marriage? Whatever it is, being fully on board with that will help you ride out the rough times and successfully deal with the frustrations. Similarly, in your relationship with your golf swing, unless you have unfettered intent and can commit fully to striking the ball, you might still have a good day, but it will most likely be filled with bad golf.

Commitment and trust go hand in hand. Before you can fully commit to the swing you're about to attempt, you must trust that such a swing actually exists for you—at this particular time. It's all about being able to fully embrace what's happening now. You'll only believe you have the swing a particular shot calls for if you've practiced it enough to trust that you can be successful executing it.

In marriage, you can similarly develop the confidence to be committed and trusting if you've put in the time working on your technique, practicing how to execute successfully in a wide range of circumstances.

In golf, you need to go out and create those circumstances when you practice. In marriage, don't worry—they'll be created for you.

Bad marriages and bad golf happen to good people all the time—it's the norm—but anyone can learn how to handle the tough times better if you're willing to put some time and effort into understanding what's actually happening to you.

Honeymoon

Wife: Honey, do you remember how much fun we had on our honeymoon?

Husband: Sure, how could I ever forget it?
I broke ninety the second day we were there.

Chapter 2

Your Fate Is Decided

Think long and hard before you get married.
—Clint Eastwood

*Golf puts a man's character on the anvil and his richest qualities—
patience, poise, and restraint—to the flame."*
—Billy Casper

**Deciding to play golf or to get married can be like entering the
event horizon of a black hole. Get ready for some weird stuff.**

How well you play golf and how well you do marriage
ultimately depends on what you're about, and how you relate
what you're about to your surroundings and interactions. In
other words, the quality of your experience reflects who you are
and what you're attempting to do with your life.

The most important question to answer prior to getting
married is simply, "Why am I doing this?" The answer you give
to this question establishes your intent, which needs to have
enough heft to support you through times that may seem very
strange to you.

For golf, one would think knowing your intent when choosing
to play would be easier than understanding your intent when

getting married. As with marriage, there are many reasons why you might choose to take up golf. You might choose to play because you know it's very hard and you just want to challenge yourself (I hope that's not the reason you decided to get married), or you might choose to play for many other reasons, like sucking up to your boss or hanging out with friends. Whatever your reason for deciding to tee it up, your fate is sealed, because the day will surely come when you ask yourself, "Why?!"

The good news is, every time you play there will be lots of opportunities to help you learn more about the person swinging that golf club. Establishing this approach to your golf can also pay dividends with your marriage, to the extent you can make it habit to handle your marriage relationship in a similar way.

After you've thought long and hard, you might choose to get married because it seems like a good idea at the time, or because you really want to make yourself and another human being happy. Whatever it is you're attempting to deal with when you decide to get married (or play golf), when the frustrations start building, think back and remind yourself of those reasons.

There are many reasons people choose to marry: love, emotional security or insecurity, intimacy, loneliness, the search for happiness, children, religion, material power, political power, folly, etc., etc. Believe it or not, here in the twenty-first century there are still people in the world who marry just for the sex (as the old saying goes, marrying for sex is like buying an airline for the free pretzels) but I guess any reason is better than none at all.

Whatever it is you're trying to do for yourself by getting married, be aware of it and take full ownership of it. Unless you got yourself caught up in a shotgun wedding, you're getting married because you choose to do so. Try to be fully aware and completely honest about why you're making that choice. If you can't clearly explain to yourself why you're getting married, it's probably a good idea to take a few more laps around the dating scene until a good reason comes to mind.

The marriage decision is like the old chicken-or-egg question. Are you looking to get married because you're ready for the commitment and now just need to find the right person? Or did you happen to meet someone so wonderful that you're moved to take that big step and marry them so they don't get away? Probably more marriage decisions fall in the latter category, especially for younger couples. Whichever way it happens for you, there remains the big question of whether or not you and this person are a good fit for each other. Usually only time and experience can answer that question (no matter how many matchmaking forms you fill out).

Whatever your reasons for taking up golf, thinking about why you are doing it is useful if you want to get the full measure of the experiences golf offers. Giving some thought to why you decided to play will help you maintain a healthy and balanced perspective when all of your reasoning is defied (and it ultimately will be). No matter what got you going in the sport, if you expect it to be a wild and crazy challenge and take on a "Damn the torpedoes—full speed ahead!" attitude, you'll be more likely to hang in there and let it continue to give you what the sport has to offer. As I like to remind my friends, I've had some bad scores, but I've never had a bad day playing golf.

Chapter 3

Learning to Hit
Teaches How Not to Hit

*Never yet have I experienced from the fair sex
such energetic rejection of all advances.*
—Albert Einstein

*It took me seventeen years to get three thousand hits in baseball.
I did it in one afternoon on the golf course.*
—Hank Aaron

Men like hitting things. In golf, your frustration comes from the difficulty in learning how to hit. In marriage, it can be equally frustrating learning how not to hit (physically and otherwise).

It's all about relationships. According to a celebrated seventy-five-year study completed at Harvard University a few years ago, it's mostly the quality and warmth of relationships you have that will determine your long-term life satisfaction and longevity.

If you're a married person who also happens to be a golfer, you have at least two important relationships in your life: the one with your spouse, and the one with your golf swing. Both

19

relationships make similar demands on you and need to be nurtured and developed if you want to find and stay in touch with the happy person that everyone has somewhere inside.

Improve your golf by getting a better understanding of that unique set of personal characteristics you need to apply to the task of consistently hitting the ball in the direction of the green. Then, realize it's that same person responding to similarly difficult challenges in your marriage relationship. If you can figure out how to deal with the you that can't seem to avoid shanking short irons or yipping three-foot putts, you can employ that same skill set when your partner does or says something you can't believe an adult person would say or do. The shanks and yips you experience in golf come from the same kind of self-control issues that can generate bitterness and strife in your marriage.

What It Takes

To *hit* a golf ball	To *not hit* your spouse
Learn to relate to your physical, mental, and emotional systems as a dynamic unit.	Learn to relate to your physical, mental, and emotional systems as a dynamic unit.
Have solid, basic swing mechanics.	Get along with someone who is naturally, fundamentally different from you.
Manage expectations.	Manage expectations.
Find peace with your unique set of personal demons.	Find peace with *two* unique sets of personal demons.
Learn to be okay with and prosper from adversity.	Learn to be okay with and prosper from adversity.

Learn to embrace change and work with it as a natural and inevitable occurrence.	Learn to embrace change and work with it as a natural and inevitable occurrence.
Avoid the trap of trying to buy a swing by frequently changing equipment.	Avoid the trap of demanding that your spouse take ownership of your happiness.
Understand the importance of small things.	Understand the importance of small things.
Keep the focus on having fun.	Make a habit of accentuating the positive.

Since there is so much similarity between the skills needed to hit a golf ball and those needed to not hit your spouse, if you can successfully do the things in the golf list, maybe you'll stand a good chance of achieving the ones on the marriage side. Your golf score will show how well connected you are with yourself, while your marriage will test how well you can stay connected.

There are many different strategies you can use to help you work with this. For example, some might choose to have a beer or two to get into a more relaxed state of mind to help them reduce tension (the chemical induction approach). Others find it useful to get away and be with their thoughts (the man-cave approach). Speaking of man caves: Ben Hogan, one of the greatest and most revered professional golfers of all time, at one point allegedly kept a separate apartment so he could retreat to his own space from time to time. He loved his wife, but he needed the man cave to help keep that love renewed.

But both approaches provide only temporary relief. Once the buzz wears off, or once you come out of the man cave, all the challenges you were escaping from are right there to welcome you back for another dose of frustration.

Both lists above, the learn-to-hit and the learn-to-not-hit, have more to do with you than with things outside you.

One of the most important of the requirements listed is that of learning to deal with change. Just when you think you have your relationship understood, something changes that re-introduces challenge. For example, let's say after a few years of marital bliss (and maybe a baby or two) you, your spouse, or both of you experience a large increase in BMI (body mass index). You might think this should be an inconsequential change, but in both your marriage and your golf-swing relationship you'll probably have to make some kind of adjustment (mental, physical, or both) to return the relationship to the pre-change state. In golf, a BMI increase alters the optimal tempo and balance dynamic you have with your golf swing. In marriage, such a change tends to mess with your focus and your attitude.

Change is unavoidable and can bring you closer together, or it can send you further apart.

Whenever you change, your relationship with your golf swing will change as well. Depending on where the relationship was prior to the change, in terms of your golf score the net result might be good, or it might be bad. Golf is so sensitive to your mind-body-spirit system that small changes can make a big difference. Awareness of this is a key to having a consistently strong golf-swing relationship.

One of the best ways to deal with change in either your golf or marriage relationship is to expect it to happen. You may not be able to see it coming or anticipate its nature, but if you accept the inevitability of change, you'll be ahead of the game.

Snowball's Chance

A guy stood over his tee shot for a long time. Finally his playing partner says, "Well, are you going to tee off or not?"

The guy answers, "My wife's up there watching me from the clubhouse. I want to make this a perfect shot."

"Forget it, man. You don't stand a snowball's chance in hell of hitting her from here."

Chapter 4

Do You Know What You're Doing?

I'm in love with a woman I can't stand!
—Richard Pryor

They say golf is like life, but don't believe them.
It's much more complicated than that.
—G. Dickinson

The more you understand the work needed to perfect your golf swing, the better you'll understand the work needed to perfect your marriage.

Once you reach the point where you're comfortable with what you're attempting to do on the golf course, the course may well become your go-to refuge from the daily stresses of life. The key here is *being comfortable with what you're attempting to do*. If you're out there trying to show the game who's boss, your golf-swing relationship will simply replace one type of stress with another—and the course becomes no refuge at all.

In golf, for the ninety-five percent of us who are right-handed, we must learn to get the left side of the body out of the way in order to have a smooth follow-through when the right side comes across. In marriage, for one hundred percent of us, we must learn to get the left side of the brain out of the way in order to manage a smooth emotional follow-through and develop the give-and-take rhythm that's needed.

Playing good golf requires the development of dynamic meditation skills. There are elements of both physics and metaphysics at play as you trundle and bash your way around the course's eighteen holes. Each attempt to advance the ball is a unique event in space-time, because never again will all the things that affect the outcome combine in exactly the same way. A serious player will spend his or her entire golfing life (which, hopefully, will coincide with his or her entire biological life) trying to develop a swing that can hold all mental, physical, and emotional obstacles at bay for that brief two or three seconds it takes to strike the ball. For many of us, though, it seems the harder we try, the worse we get.

It's the same with marriage. We try to learn to process what we're feeling in our mental, physical, and emotional spaces before responding to what our spouse just said or did. More and more, integrative science is working to put together IQ (mental intelligence), EQ (emotional intelligence), and what my wife calls BQ (body intelligence—recognizing the physiological signals your body gives you when it's stressed) as a unified self-management challenge.

But for now, from time to time it seems that no matter what we say or do, it only makes things worse. Learning to instantaneously get into that dynamic meditation state on the golf course will also pay off in the ability to handle a marriage challenge without worsening the situation.

In golf, you need to get in touch with the core of your soul and achieve solace with what you find there. Then, if what you find there happens to be preventing you from achieving your best golf swing, you need to muster the strength and courage to change whatever it is. You achieve this through many cycles of practice and reflection.

Your marriage will force you to do the same thing and likely send you back to seek an even deeper level of work. Golf offers infinite levels of developmental opportunity. No matter how often you feel the need to head off to what is essentially an emotional proving ground, there's always the chance to come back a better man or woman.

When you've matured as a golfer and learned to find pleasure in a day of bogies as well as a day of birdies, you might then be ready for what has been called the most difficult, and most fun, task of all: reacting with kindness and love when your spouse gives you a hard time for going to the golf course instead of doing something he or she wanted you to do (e.g. mowing the lawn)!

Recent studies have shown that in the United States, both traditional marriage and eighteen-hole golf games have declined somewhat in popularity. The trend is most apparent for those under the age of thirty. This group is also less inclined to cohabit, as compared with previous generations. There's a downside to this, since studies have shown that American married men tend to live longer than their never-married or divorced counterparts. Numerous research results show married men living, on average, about seventeen years longer than single men. According to research published by the *American Journal of Sociology,* married men have a roughly twenty percent better chance of living long enough to enjoy full Social Security benefits than their single, divorced, or widowed counterparts. (And it's a double whammy for the divorced guys, who also lose a lot of money for other reasons.) It's been suggested that a major influence on this equation is the fact that married men tend to take better care of themselves and, as part of that effort, take fewer risks.

On the other hand, those same researchers found that if your marriage is particularly stressful, not only do you lose those seventeen extra years, you also see your expected lifespan shorten.

Research shows that playing golf can also give you an actuarial advantage. A major study done at a Swedish medical university found that golfers are forty percent less likely to have died than nongolfers of the same age, sex, and socioeconomic status. You might think this would have to do with the fact that golf gets you outside for some fresh air and exercise (a typical round of golf burns between 1,000 and 2,000 calories, depending on whether you ride or walk the course). However, the study also showed that it was more than just walking that provided the benefit. The actual act of playing the game made a difference. Interestingly, the study also found that blue-collar golfers enjoyed a greater health benefit than white-collar golfers. In addition, they found that the lower your handicap, the higher will be your life expectancy. (Regarding this last point, it seems likely that this is due to the fact that lower handicaps require more time on the course.) The study also suggests that factors beyond physical exercise (e.g., the social aspects of the game) may also contribute to golf's beneficial effect on health.

The study did not consider whether a bad golf-swing relationship might affect your health. It seems logical, however, that if that relationship is particularly stressful—as it may also be with your marriage—the best way to keep either from killing you is to figure out how to dial down that stress.

Both your marriage and your golf-swing relationships can be beneficial to your health, if you're able to keep those relationships relatively positive. Learning to keep it positive on the golf course can translate to the home, because both situations call on the same set of mental and emotional reflexes. Developing those reflexes in one arena also helps in the other.

I know a guy who says his technique is to force himself to laugh any time he feels sad, afraid, or disgusted. That sounds good to me, but it may not work for everyone. The key is to decide what kind of energy you want to experience at a particular instant, then do your level best to put that kind of energy out there. If you can get to a point where you begin to truly understand what you're doing, putting those reflexes in place will become much easier.

You don't fail at marriage or golf unless you choose to be untrue to your intent. If your marriage or your golf doesn't work out as you want it to or expect it to, that doesn't mean you're a failure. The situation is just telling you it might be time to take another look at what you think you're actually trying to do. Basically, both your golf-swing relationship and your marriage relationship can be viewed as tools or processes for helping you find a way to get more out of life.

Chapter 5

Ask and You Might Receive

Golf is deceptively simple and endlessly complicated;
it satisfies the soul and frustrates the intellect.
—Arnold Palmer

Expectation is the root of all heartache.
—Buddhist doctrine

Playing golf is a lot like chasing after a gorgeous woman.

If you're successful, there will probably come a time when you regret it.

The regret doesn't come from having success. Rather, it comes from the elevated expectations we tend to have as a result of that success. Here's another way of expressing the above Buddhist idea: Happiness equals Reality divided by Expectations (**H=R/E**).

Researchers say that most of our happiness is determined by the genes inherited from our parents. However, while our genes greatly dictate how we choose to deal with the challenges that come to us daily, the real element that dictates our happiness is what we expect to get out of the things we do.

I believe that men love golf and women for the same reason—the intriguing nature of beautiful complexity. It's the desire and challenge to control or master something that we know, deep down inside, cannot be completely controlled or mastered. And that's what keeps us coming back for more.

Why do we do it? Why do we marry and play golf, given how completely baffling and gut-wrenching each endeavor can be (for both men and women)? Could it be because we just don't realize at the outset how totally frustrating the experience might be? Maybe it's the ego boost we get from believing that we're in control, with the amount of the boost being in direct proportion to the size of the control challenge.

In golf as in marriage, we spend the bulk of our time trying to understand and defeat those physical, mental, and emotional obstacles that can stand in the way of happiness. It seems that the higher our performance-expectation level, the greater will be the number and size of the obstacles that appear. If you expect your spouse to forever remain the physical '10' he or she was when you married, you should prepare for eventual disappointment. If you expect your tee shot to fly straight and true for 250 yards every time, you'll probably be disappointed on most days. At some point, staying happy might require you to be okay with a spouse who has become an 8 or even a 6, and a tee shot that makes it out 200 yards or so before fading into the rough.

Figuring out what you're expecting and why you're expecting it will help you. In golf, it makes sense to have rising expectations for your game as your ability to strike the ball consistently improves. In this case, reality is going up along with your expectations, so happiness is maintained. In marriage, as your relationship develops, your expectations might rise in concert with reality, provided you're not focusing so much on the things that excited you during the dating phase.

There are consultants and online dating and matchmaking companies that, for a price, will give you an impressive matrix with dozens of personality parameters to help you construct the supposedly correct personality type for marriage consideration. More important than trying to find the ideal personality is, however, simply embracing the realization, and understanding the implications surrounding that realization, that there are fundamental differences between men and women as designed by nature.

Accepting this is key to setting your expectations before committing to something you're not ready for. No matter how many squares get checked off on your potential-partner decision matrix, there are basic gender-based differences that, sooner or later, will come into play around some of the issues that push your reaction buttons very hard. Also, the way you fill out that form today will be different from the way you might fill it out in one, five, or ten years from now—as your expectations, patience, maturity, and other characteristics change over time.

The good news is, you can learn to handle this process in ways that are positive for the relationship.

Generally speaking, men and women tend to internalize inputs from the world around them in different ways. Men tend naturally to define and arrive at solutions by subscribing to what I call the Aristotelian way of connecting the dots. Women, on the other hand, might prefer to "feel" around for what might work, which could lead to a conclusion totally opposite to the one arrived at by a man. Ideally, we would value both approaches and stand ready to implement either in any given situation. In cases where neither approach is sufficient on its own, some combination of the two might be in order. Still, there will be times when both partners will need to rein in their egos and continue to struggle—as partners—to find the best solution.

Some women fall into the trap of marrying an alpha male, then expect him to make her the most important thing in his life forever. What she needs to understand is that, more often than not, and especially these days, the alpha male *is* the alpha male because *he* has been the most important thing in his life. Having high expectations for yourself or your partner is great, but remember: The higher you set them, the higher will be the chances that you'll have to deal with more frustration.

When setting your expectations for married life, keep in mind that your partner will probably never again look as good as he or she does on your wedding day, and the sex will probably never again be as exciting as it is on your honeymoon. And it's not just the physical side of things that you'll need to make allowances for, but most aspects of your relationship: Communication, preferred living style, perceptions, attitudes, desires and needs, etc., are all likely to hit points of crisis sooner or later. Expect this and prepare.

In golf, there is a honeymoon during that brief period when, as a newbie, you're okay with not being able to play the game well. After all, you're a beginner and don't yet have high expectations. Then an interesting thing happens. You get hooked on the absolute, insanity-inducing challenge of trying to strike the ball and have it go where you want it to. The more competitive you are, the further you get sucked into the madness. Eventually most golfers settle into one of two attitudes. They either relax about it, learning to enjoy a day away from the office and finding satisfaction with the prospect of never being able to break seventy, eighty, ninety, or maybe even a hundred. Or else they curse the day they picked up a golf club, and with a great sense of relief, sell their gear at a yard sale or banish it to the deepest recess of a closet or garage to collect dust for all time. A third option would be to find satisfaction in continuing to work on the small inner things that stand in the way breaking eighty or ninety. The expectations you come to have for your golf game will determine which of these scenarios becomes your own.

Similarly, in marriage, most will eventually either choose to get out of the marriage, or else readjust the expectations they have for their spouse. As with golf, a third option here would be to get hooked on the challenge of working on all the little things that can take the relationship to a higher level. This could involve taking another long hard look at your original intent, in relation to what you believe will make you happy today.

Ed and Nancy

Ed and Nancy met on a cruise ship, and Ed was immediately taken with Nancy's beauty and personality.

When they discovered that they lived a few miles apart, Ed was ecstatic.

He immediately started asking her out when they got home. Within a few weeks Ed had taken Nancy to dance clubs, restaurants, concerts, movies, and museums. Each date seemed better than the last, and Ed became convinced that Nancy was his soul mate and true love.

On the one-month anniversary of their first dinner on the cruise ship, Ed took Nancy to a fine restaurant. While having cocktails and waiting for their salad, Ed said, "I guess you can tell I'm very much in love with you. I'd like a little serious talk before our relationship continues to the next stage. So, before I get a box out of my jacket and ask you a life-changing question, it's only fair to warn you that I'm a total golf nut. I play golf, I read about golf, I watch golf on TV. In short, I eat, sleep, and breathe golf. If that's going to be a problem for us, you'd better say so now!"

Nancy took a deep breath and responded, "Ed, that certainly won't be a problem. I love you as you are, and I love golf, too.

However, since we're being totally honest with each other, you need to know that for the last five years I've been a hooker."

Ed said, "I'll bet it's because you're bending you wrists slightly when you hit the ball."

Chapter 6

Make Adversity Your Adventure

Marriage is our last, best chance to grow up.
— Joseph Barth

I tried harder and harder but played worse and worse!
—Jesper Parnevik

In golf and in marriage, adversity happens much of the time. If you can learn to turn that adversity into adventure, you can resolve your troubles at a much lower cost.

Many performance experts believe that becoming an expert at any physical skill generally requires about 10,000 hours of practice. Most golfers who quit the game (for the first time) do so after only two or three years. Assuming that the 10,000-hour rule is correct, and that the average beginner puts in about ten hours per week on developing his or her golf swing, that means it should take about twenty years to achieve expert status. There are a host of reasons why most people don't make it to the 10,000-hour point in golf, but I believe the biggest is that golf is such an uncommonly and emotionally taxing thing to do.

Marriage is a 24/7 proposition, which means you hit the 10,000-hour point after a little more than a year. As it turns out, most marriages that end in divorce do so after about 60,000 hours—six times the amount of effort that should get you to the expert level. But perhaps, once you've become an expert at it, you realize that you shouldn't have done it in the first place. Or it could be that people hang in there longer than they should because there's a much higher penalty for failure.

Probably the best way to find satisfaction in an environment where your relationship with your emotions is constantly being tested is to decide that you're going to view those agitations as learning opportunities (what I call the failure-is-food model), then look for the benefit they can bring as you develop the skill to recognize and appreciate that benefit.

In golf, making adventure out of adversity means learning that you can have a bad hole or a bad round and still manage to have a great day. In marriage, it means having a bad day and then figuring out how that can help you have a better marriage.

For most, the love-hate relationship that exists with both marriage and golf is totally logical, given the nature of men, women, and golf. The idea is to figure out how to get through a day of experience with your spouse or your golf swing without getting so frustrated that you build up what we might call a potentially terminal level of resentment or depression. The adversity is there for guys (men being the natural calculators they are) because after logically connecting all the dots, they just can't understand how the outcome got so screwed up.

I know a guy who has only half of his golf clubs in his bag. The other half are in the lake at his favorite course. He says he got rid of the clubs because he just "can't hit them anymore so, what use are they?" Throwing your clubs in the lake is a high price to pay, materially and otherwise. One reason for this is because you're letting adversity get the best of you, denying you the benefit of the adventure. It happens to every golfer. One day you're hitting clubs like a champ, the next you're hitting them like a chump, and it's a guessing game as to what will happen when you make your swing. It makes you want to scream, "Hey, can't we just get along ?!"

In marriage, the equivalent of tossing your clubs in the lake is something that will probably turn out to be a lot more expensive, and you don't want that.

Along with golf, we go into marriage with high enthusiasm and anticipation, only to find that both are too hard and unnatural for the average person. You might throw lots of money at the problem, hiring swing coaches, marriage counselors, therapists, hypnotists, witch doctors, and other experts who try to cure your slice or bring back marital bliss. These professionals can help in many cases (good outside help can be a key to success), especially with the mechanical basics of golf or the communication basics of marriage. But in the end, whether or not you eventually toss your clubs or quit your marriage will be determined by how well you learn to make adversity work for you.

As it turns out, the main difference between adversity and adventure is how we interpret the situation, and what we believe about our ability to deal with it. In golf, if you've hit the shot before, you know it's in you. You just have to figure out how to dial it up on command. The situation can then be experienced as an opportunity to increase your skill level. If you haven't had the experience of successfully hitting this shot before, you've probably seen it hit by someone else (a touring professional, perhaps), so you know it can be done. It then becomes a matter of embracing the challenge of learning what it takes to execute the necessary swing.

Marriage is very similar. If you're angry or agitated about some marital experience, in all likelihood that experience stirs your feelings in a way that is not entirely unique in your relationship. Since you figured out how to get through it (or something similar to it) before, you believe you can do it again, perhaps by paying particular attention to what it took to move things forward the last time this happened. If, on the other hand, it's the first time you've had to deal with such a situation in your marriage, you do the same thing you'd do in golf: study how others have successfully handled the issue, if possible, then try the approach that worked for them to improve your skill in dealing with the same situation.

To form the habit of taking adversity to adventure, you have to be willing to view the problem objectively and consider it to be as much about you as anything or anyone else. After missing that two-foot putt that would have won the tournament, it's easy to swear at your putter before ceremoniously tossing it into the lake. Likewise in marriage, it's easy to place the blame on your spouse, then walk away to let him or her stew in guilt. In both cases, though, you'll miss the opportunity to extract adventure from adversity, because you've run away from it instead.

Chapter 7

Your Demons Love You

Golf ... is the infallible test. The man who can go into a patch of rough alone, with the knowledge that only God is watching him, and play his ball where it lies is the man who will serve you faithfully and well.
— P. G. Wodehouse

The mind is its own place, and in itself,
can make a Heaven of Hell, a Hell of Heaven.
—Milton

The source of frustration, exasperation, and fear in your marriage is the same as it is in your golf game. You can handle them both the same way.

After a complete physical exam, my doctor once said to me, "I recommend that you either call off the wedding or play more golf." He gave me that recommendation as we toiled to understand why, for the first time in my life, I was beset with severe insomnia.

After a long and fun-filled bachelor life, I had recently become engaged to be married. I was, in my mind, convinced that this was the right time and the right woman. A few weeks after we announced our engagement, I found that I couldn't sleep at night. It was the beginning of May, and the wedding was set for November!

After conducting the obligatory battery of tests designed to rule out any physical pathology, my doctor just threw up his hands and made the above statement. Since both my family and that of my wife-to-be were very excited about our pending nuptials (we'd both waited fairly late in life to get married) and wedding preparations were speedily being made, I decided the most prudent course of action would be the latter—I played more golf. Eventually, my insomnia subsided and I was able to sleep normally before the day of the wedding.

Whether it was the golf that did it, the meditation, the green tee, the massages, or just time to settle down, I'm not sure. But I do know it was one of the strangest and most frightening experiences I've ever had. I believe that what happened to me in this instance was basically a subconscious panic attack. Consciously, I felt completely ready and totally prepared, both mentally and emotionally, for marriage. But clearly, somewhere deep inside, there was grave concern.

Getting cold feet before taking wedding vows is fairly common. We've all heard the stories where either the bride-to-be or the groom-to-be is a no-show on the wedding day, leaving the other shocked and embarrassed while waiting at the altar. I'm sure any competent psychologist would be able to give a lengthy explanation of this phenomenon and explain what's likely to be going on in the absentee partner's mind when such things happen. In my view, it harks back to a basic life principle: The importance of the decision you're making directly affects the degree of comfort and understanding you can achieve about who you really are and what you really want from life.

Decision-wise, it may be less important to determine whether or not to play golf than it is to decide whether or not to get married—but the two decisions can be comparable in terms of what you eventually learn about yourself. Getting the deal you want from the things you do is very closely tied to how much you know and accept about yourself before you take action.

In the classic sci-fi thriller *Forbidden Planet*, Dr. Morbius ultimately realizes that the power source of the great demon attacking his fortress is his own mind.

Often, in marriage and in golf, we perceive our circumstances to be an existential struggle that forces us to look into the mirror of our souls and try coming to grips with what we find there. Sometimes, when we examine critically what we think we want to be, the most undesirable aspects of who we are come to light. One way to help is to stop thinking about all the bad stuff that can happen if we screw up.

I have a simple formula for the golf swing: $Sc = Sp + M$. Sc is the swing that counts (i.e., you're trying to advance the ball to the green and make par or better), Sp is your practice swing, and M is what I call the mental engagement factor. This formula demands that the greater the mental engagement, the greater will be the distortion of the swing that counts (Sc) as compared with your practice swing (Sp). Therefore, the thing we must learn to do is just to let the swing happen, instead of trying to force it to happen. In other words, have that M-factor move as close to zero as possible by getting your mind out of the way.

For marriage, the analogous formula is $R = M + B$. In this formula, R is your response to the "weird" thing your spouse just said or did, M represents your reason for being married in the first place, and B is what I call the battle factor. The battle factor represents the degree to which your ego wants to show this person who's boss. This formula says that the more successful you are at minimizing the effect of B (the battle factor), the more your response will reflect the original intent you had for your marriage—the most desired response.

An important thing to be aware of with both golf and marriage is that you are (when viewed from a purely rational or mechanical perspective) choosing to enter a realm of wonderful and massive complexity. Consequently, you have to learn to be okay with being wrong more often than you think is fair. Being wrong in this case doesn't necessarily mean you miscalculated and therefore committed an error, but rather that your efforts are simply being rejected by forces you don't completely understand, see clearly, or believe to make sense.

Having this awareness will allow you to go deeper into understanding what you're dealing with and allow you to improve your relationship with both your golf swing and your spouse. This is important because it helps you build a habit of positive response, which can ultimately keep frustration levels from rising too high. If the frustration level gets too high, it usually leads the frustrated one to look for a quick way out of the situation, when it can be more productive and fulfilling over the long term to work things through and achieve a higher level of ability.

For any given challenging situation, in marriage or golf, too much time spent pondering a response (e.g., thinking about how to hit a shot in golf, or thinking about how to win an argument in marriage) can cause the situation to spiral downward. This, in turn, can increase the level of agitation in your marriage relationship and broaden the error footprint in your golf-swing relationship. Some teaching professionals use the phrase "automatic golf" when referring to the point where you achieve the best time delay (unique to your own swing) between setup and swing initiation. Similarly, we might use the term "automatic marriage" for the point at which you achieve that response timing sweet spot with your loved one.

It's Not Working

I came home from the golf course today. My wife had left a note on the refrigerator: "IT'S NOT WORKING, I can't take it anymore... gone to stay with my mother!!"

I opened the fridge, the light came on, and the beer was cold. What the hell is she talking about????

Chapter 8

Habits, Not Equipment, Make the Man

*Golf and sex are about the only things you can enjoy
without being good at it.*
—Jimmy Demaret

*After marriage, husband and wife become two sides of a coin;
they just can't face each other, but still they stay together.*
—Hemant Joshi

**If you make your golf swing or your marriage relationship a
contest—believe me, you will lose!**

You use the golf swing to advance the ball toward your goal—
getting on the green and into the cup. In marriage, the golf
swing's equivalent can be found in your habits, and in the
attitude you have about your relationship with this other
person. In marriage, the nature of your relationship advances
you toward your combined life goals (lasting love, happy
family, etc.) and is dictated by those habits and attitudes. If you
find yourself always thinking win-lose when faced with a
marriage-relationship challenge, that's analogous to what they
call fighting your swing in golf. If this becomes habit, it will

make turmoil the normal state of your marriage or golf-swing relationship.

One of the best ways to develop a mindset that supports positive outcomes is to learn to internalize every problem situation as a unique opportunity. Every time you successfully get through one of these situations, you increase your skill set for dealing with the next, possibly bigger challenge. As your marriage and your golf game develop, the challenges you confront in each will get bigger.

Let's say you just hit your ball into the lake adjacent to the eighteenth green, after having had a pretty good round up to that point. What about the way you handle that situation can you apply when, say, your spouse just screwed up this month's budget by putting some crazy purchase on the credit card?

Moving into contest mode with your next ball will just increase the likelihood that you'll drop a third, because now you're trying to prove that you have the ability to overpower whatever it was that caused you to hit the first ball into the lake. It would be better to step back, maybe have a chuckle, then take a few long, slow, deep breaths and bring some positive energy back into your mental, physical, and emotional state. Reducing fear and tension will instantly reset the relationship with your golf swing. And by emotionally accepting what just happened instead of being offended by it, you'll be better prepared to execute the next attempt.

With marriage, this same approach will help you to come up with alternatives to fight-or-flight and turn the episode into an experience that strengthens the relationship. For the most part, this is dictated by attitude—which determines how you feel about these situations, just as your habits determine how you act about them.

Knowing how and when to change a habit is one of life's greatest wisdoms. Unfortunately, changing a habit is also one of life's most difficult things to do. One way to think of habits is to see them as a kind of reflex that grows into our subconscious, or what you might call emotional muscle memory.

Let's say you get some manner of stimulus or input from your spouse—for example, he or she says something you internalize as sarcastic, irritating, or idiotic. And you react to it in the way you have so many times before, by getting angry or telling your spouse how stupid it was to say or do that. Then, after a few cycles of back-and-forth point-counterpoint, you wind up with an argument, hurt feelings, emotional withdrawal, and a cloud of negativity. That's one type of habitual response.

Another might be a response where you don't initially say anything, but you're thinking to yourself, *What an idiot!* or *How did I ever wind up married to this person?* In that case, the outward argument doesn't initially take place, but you still end up with the same effect on the relationship. These are just two possibilities chosen from a broad range of habitual responses that such a situation might generate.

A different response—and one that might do the relationship some good (by generating the least amount of negative energy and tension)—is one that would have you taking a moment to process internally what you just experienced before responding to it. Not just thinking about what was said or done, but checking in with what gets activated inside you because of it.

In the second response above, you take time to denigrate your spouse in your mind before responding, which is actually a step in the right direction since you don't immediately start an argument fueled by emotion. On the other hand, you don't want bad feelings to fester for too long, because that could build up tension and keep you from successfully talking it out later.

The next step would be to move away from denigration altogether and focus more on what you're feeling and how to deal with that. You develop this habit over time, by reminding yourself before something happens that when you feel that impulse to react in the negative, you will instead wait a few seconds and do some processing of what you feel and why you feel it, before responding. Each morning, remind yourself (perhaps while brushing your teeth or having breakfast) that you will not immediately react when your wife or husband says or does something that ticks you off. The simple act of coaching yourself about this will help you break the habit of knee-jerk reactions. Most of the time, those angry responses set you back a stroke or two anyway.

When something angers you, cultivate the habit of expressing your feelings in a nonthreatening way, instead of acting on that anger out of habit. Practice the skill of expressing your anger in ways that are clear and nonthreatening. You might even use humor, when appropriate. Make a habit of talking about how you feel and suggesting possible solutions that will work for you.

Creating a new habit starts with a conscious decision to do it. The next step is finding the right routine to minimize the difficulty of doing it. Some habits come about fairly easily, because they seem like the natural thing to do. Those habits require little conscious effort, and you feel discomfort right away if you don't do them (e.g., lining up the ball before making your putt). Other habits—usually the most important ones—require that we take more time and be more conscious of our effort, because the discomfort comes when we attempt to do them (e.g., inviting directions from your wife when you get lost).

Research has shown that it can take at least three to four weeks to create a new habit. In most cases it can actually take longer than that (anywhere from a few weeks to a few months or more), depending on what you're working on, how you're working on it, and your personality. For various reasons, creating habits for your golf game generally takes a bit less time than creating habits for your marriage.

One habit you will come up with during the development of your golf game is a set of movements and thinking that are part of what's called the pre-shot routine. This important settling-down process represents your unique mind-body preparation for the execution of your swing. The pre-shot routine should help you to relax and get mentally and emotionally centered prior to starting the swing motion. Some people wag the club several times; some folks wag their butts or do a little dance; some whistle a tune (Jack Nicklaus has been known to do this) or just take a few deep breaths and envision the ball in flight.

The practice swing is a key part of your pre-shot routine. You use the practice swing to get a feel for what it's like for your body to move in a way that will put the ball on the desired flight trajectory. Some people always take two practice swings. Others take three or (hopefully not in your foursome) more. However many practice swings it takes, you shouldn't attempt to strike the ball until your swing feels comfortable.

An effective pre-shot routine will help you get quickly to the low emotional-energy state (I call it centering) required for your body to execute the golf swing as purely and smoothly as possible.

There are about as many different pre-shot routines as there are golfers. Some people can get caught in what you might call a pre-shot routine do-loop. This is where their mind-body subsystem basically plays "hot potato" with the swing trigger, handing it back and forth and causing a kind of dithering or oscillation to take place between those two nodes. This dithering results in the golfer spending an inordinate amount of time standing over the ball, causing tension to develop and making it that much more difficult to execute a proper swing. Though the purpose of the pre-shot routine is to minimize or eliminate tension, it can actually become a source of tension if it gets out of control.

In marriage you must work to develop what I like to call the pre-*shout* routine, which serves the same function in marriage that the pre-shot routine does in golf. When facing a situation with your spouse, you need to have a habit that allows you to settle and center yourself and achieve that low emotional-energy state before responding or acting on what's happening. Wagging your butt probably won't help in this case, though there are surely exceptions. And so the marital equivalent of butt-wagging might be something like counting to ten, envisioning a placid scene, taking a short walk, or doing something else that puts a little temporal distance between what your spouse said or did and what you eventually say or do about it. As with the practice swing in the pre-shot golf routine, in the marriage pre-shout routine, if what you're about to say or do doesn't feel like it will make the situation better—don't execute it. You should think again and come up with something that feels like it will help the situation.

To achieve a golf swing that is repeatable, energy efficient, adaptable, etc., and to build the desired automatic response for those challenging situations with your spouse, you have to work on the right things. For golf, work to develop proper muscle memory (a.k.a. procedural memory or implicit memory), so you're not fighting your large muscle groups each time you step up to the tee. For both golf and marriage, learn to savor the moment and to achieve what I call instantaneous centering, so that when you make your swing or communicate your response to your spouse, it increases the likelihood that the next action you take will move you toward the green or it's marriage equivalent. Instantaneous centering is the ability to achieve, within a few seconds, an emotional-energy state that is low enough for you to act in a way that is not distorted or distracted by fear or doubt. You must first believe that you can do this, then do the work to eventually get it to a point where it becomes habit.

Miss Her

Bill: My wife says she's leaving me if I don't give up golf.

Bob: What are you going to do?

Bill: Miss her like hell.

Chapter 9

We're Talking About Practice, Man—Practice!

A successful marriage requires falling in love many times,
always with the same person.
—Mignon McLaughlin

There is no such thing as natural touch.
Touch is something you create by hitting millions of golf balls.
—Lee Trevino

To be good at golf you have to take the time to hit huge numbers of balls.

To be good at marriage you need the balls to take a huge number of hits.

The ball-hits of marriage can come at you from so many angles and intensities that you sometimes wonder what is real.

Form becomes substance at the Zen boundary, and turning form into substance is what practice is all about. More substance in your golf game means improved scores and greater enjoyment on the course. More substance in your marriage means better sex, less stress, better communications - and more golf!

Most of the top professional golfers hit hundreds of balls a day as they work on all the various phases of the game that bring a unique challenge to their golf-swing relationship. Even though most amateur golfers are satisfied with just striking the ball well enough to enjoy the round and harbor no illusions of ever joining the pro circuit, it's still necessary to put in the time at the practice range—for whatever level of ability you want to achieve. Practice will build those habits we spoke of previously, and those habits will in turn build success.

No doubt the amount of time and effort you put into practice is important. Remember, though, *what* you are practicing is even more important than *how often* you practice. If you spend several hours a day practicing bad habits and poor technique, all you'll wind up doing is firming up your golf or marriage incompetence.

In marriage, the equivalent of hundreds of balls a day at the practice range comes in the form of the things you do (or try to do) to gain a better understanding of what works with your spouse. You help that along by welcoming interactions that you, as a matter of habit, might not otherwise have. Or by being more receptive to those things your spouse will ask you to do when you're not really in the mood. You might even be proactive and surprise him or her by suggesting some of those things yourself (watching a chick flick, for example, or inviting the in-laws over for dinner).

Practice QE (qualitative easing). This is where you work on your ability to explain things to your partner in ways that make it easier for him or her to understand what you're actually trying to say. With qualitative easing, you try to ease up on the strictness of the communication style that is most natural for you, and instead work on meeting your spouse halfway by using terms, style, cadence, etc. that relate well to his or her style of communication. Maybe it's been your style to use terms that, while normal and unthreatening to you, seem demanding, controlling, or accusatory to your spouse. Such terms might tend to put him or her on the defensive and have an immediate downside effect on the quality of your communications. A simple change in some of that terminology could make a huge difference in your ability to resolve important issues.

For example, let's say your wife comes home from the office very upset with a coworker and proceeds to tell you what happened. After giving her more than thirty seconds to explain how she's feeling, instead of saying "Why didn't you say this, why didn't you do that, blah, blah, blah...?" you might say, "What do you think about blah, blah, blah...?" Or be even more empathetic by inviting her to continue explaining so you can get a better understanding of the situation.

Practice allows you to tighten up your error distribution (or error footprint). The following figure is one way to picture this. Distribution (A) shows what happens with little or no practice. The (B) curve represents a moderate amount of practice. The (C) distribution happens only with lots of practice.

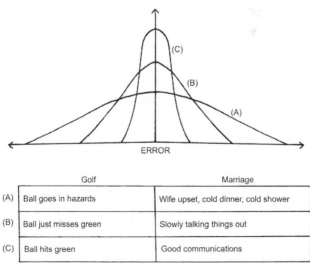

	Golf	Marriage
(A)	Ball goes in hazards	Wife upset, cold dinner, cold shower
(B)	Ball just misses green	Slowly talking things out
(C)	Ball hits green	Good communications

Figure C

Deepak Chopra says, "Nature's intelligence functions with effortless ease ... with carefreeness, harmony, and love." This is exactly where we would like our practice to take us with our golf swings and with our marriage. Getting to the point of effortless ease, carefreeness, harmony, and love requires a willingness to take the necessary time to build the habits and the reflexes that can get us there.

The more balls you hit, the deeper will be your understanding that the same bad stuff can happen over and over again, whether you think you know why it's happening or not. It's this understanding that is the essence of the benefit you get from practice. It's okay that bad stuff still happens, as long as it happens less often and with less downside impact than before. As it is with golf, so it is with marriage.

To practice golf, you get a bucket of balls and just whack away, while trying to incorporate some basic ideas about how a golf swing is supposed to work. You're actually not practicing hitting the ball, you're practicing making a golf swing. Eventually you're able to hit the ball because you're able to make a golf swing and just let the club pass through the position of the ball.

In marriage, each time you have a problem, you can make it a practice session by telling yourself, *Hey, this is just practice.* That's it! Just tell yourself this is practice. Along with that, you can also count to ten, take six deep breaths, or do some other calming thing—but remember to tell yourself that this is practice! No worries about what you're practicing for, or how the endgame will look. In time, you'll find yourself actually moving toward that effortless ease that Deepak speaks of.

Confused Caddy

After her game of golf, a lady player offered her caddy a ride into town. The caddy thankfully accepted, and when they arrived at her house, he carried her clubs inside. The lady invited him to stay for lunch and served him a wonderful meal.

She then invited him into the bedroom. He was puzzled, but went along out of curiosity. She asked if he wanted to go to bed with her, so he did that too. Later he realized it was time to get back to the course and prepared to leave. The lady golfer insisted on giving him a dollar before he could go.

This was too much for the poor man, and he asked her, "Lady, what's going on? First you feed me a delicious meal, and as if that wasn't enough, you invite me to make love to you and we have a terrific time together. Now you want to pay me?! What IS this, anyway?"

The lady explained proudly, "Well, you know Christmas is coming, and I told my husband I wanted to do something nice for my caddy, who is so faithful and helped me so much this year. And my husband said, 'Screw the caddy! Give him a dollar!' The lunch was my idea."

Chapter 10

Do You Know
Where You're Going?

Why is the game called golf?
They call it golf because all the other four-letter words were taken.
—Raymond Floyd

I asked the Lord for an angel and the Devil sent me you.
—Samson to Delilah
(from the classic Cecil B. Demille's movie)

In marriage and in golf, if you don't want to end up where you're headed, you'd better change what you're doing.

How do you know when it's time to change the way you're dealing with your marriage or your golf game? One way is to be aware that you're using more four-letter words than you did before you took up golf or got married. Another might be the realization that, much of the time, you find yourself looking forward to being somewhere else.

It's a good idea to have a destination, or what I like to think of as a clear mission, that serves the vision you have for your marriage and your golf game. Mission clarity will help you relate to all of the ups and downs that are par for the course in both golf and marriage.

When you started out in marriage or in golf, you did so with some sort of intent. At the time, you may not have been fully aware of that intent, but it was there. Mission clarity means having a strong sense of what needs to happen in order for you to move toward the goal of realizing that intent. Mission clarity also means knowing how to recognize those achievements and actions that move you in the right direction.

If you intend to stay married until death do you part, it's pretty easy to know when that's been achieved—but how can you tell if you're doing the right things to get you there? How do you recognize that your relationship is indeed moving in the desired direction? If your intent is something less than such an end-of-life objective, you need to understand how achievement of your ultimate goal (and progress toward it) is defined. Defining these things—and recognizing them when they happen—is a major challenge in marriage. It's all about getting your relationship to move in a direction that brings your intent into sharper focus.

It's easier to know when your golf-swing relationship is moving forward, because (for one thing) if it is, you can hardly wait to tee off on your next round.

The mission becomes your definition of what is needed to achieve success in a given stage of relationship development. In marriage, one stage might be helping your spouse (or yourself) to reach a point of emotional security and a higher sense of self—which is something that might take a long time to achieve. Another stage might be having children and getting a stable home environment set up. Other stages might be things like figuring out how to stay engaged after his or her first five minutes of talking, or simply being able to consistently sit down for an enjoyable dinner at home.

Getting to your intent might require many stages, or it might take only a few. It depends on the nature of the intent you have for the relationship. The key here is to have that long-term objective (represented by your intent) clearly defined in terms of smaller chunks (missions) that make it easier to know where things are headed in your relationship. If you have trouble figuring out what the various mission stages are for your relationship, you might spend more time understanding your intent and reviewing what you know about yourself and the nature of the relationship.

In golf, you also have stages of relationship development. One stage might be getting to the point where you have a repeatable swing. It doesn't have to be pretty, just repeatable. Another stage might be learning how to center instantly, or how to have a better appreciation (more sensitivity) for ball-strike feedback. Again, the key to the type and number of stages (missions) is your overall intent for your game (e.g., are you trying to turn pro, or do you just want a reason to get out of the house once a week?). Most amateur golfers are probably hoping to play well enough to be able to enjoy their outings, perhaps even impress their friends or coworkers a bit. Depending on how well your friends play, that could be a straightforward mission objective. If you reach the point of feeling like you're ready to toss your clubs into the lake, it's probably a good time to rethink both the mission and your intent.

A typical progression in golf is this: You set a goal, achieve it, and then immediately set another higher goal. That's good news, because it means that your confidence is building and you're excited about what you believe you can achieve. I know a guy who swore that all he wanted from his golf game was the ability to break ninety. But once he actually broke ninety, he decided that he should be able to break eighty. He's still trying to break eighty and routinely gets upset about not being able to meet this goal.

There's a kind of self-tyranny that comes with setting goals for your golf game, because most golfers believe they should be playing better than they do. It would be wise to view progress with your game in the same way you view progress with your marriage. Don't worry so much about getting to a specific point, just keep trying to get better each day. Set the goals and try to have mission clarity, while focusing more on how you plan to get there, rather than on when you might arrive.

When your actions aren't working, get help. Most golfers have no problem checking in with their local club pro or range instructor to get help on resolving what they believe to be a swing issue. When the instructor suggests they modify their grip or adjust their stance prior to addressing the ball, they're excited to get out to the course or range and see how those changes work. Take the same approach with your marriage: Get help. Ask for suggestions from a knowledgeable person on techniques that you might use to get your marriage back on track and rolling toward the achievement of the mission you've set for it.

Chapter 11

Maybe You Can't Dance but You Need Rhythm

Success in golf depends less on strength of body than upon strength of mind and character.
—Arnold Palmer

I love being married. It's so great to find that one special person you want to annoy for the rest of your life.
—Rita Rudner

Your golf swing has a sweet spot, and so does your marriage. Experiment with rhythm and tempo to find it.

Tempo is an important thing when solving both marriage and golf challenges. Tempo is related to a principle in physics known as resonance. For example, when a bell rings, it's ringing at its naturally resonant frequency. All physical systems have a characteristic frequency (tempo) at which they most easily and efficiently give or receive energy. In golf, this principle is related to what we call hitting the sweet spot, because it feels so sweet when your movement and impact are just right.

Having the right tempo gets you to operate at the ideal (resonant) frequency by matching the way you're built to the way you need to move. I discovered how this applied to my own body when I made an attempt to set the world record for jumping jacks. During my many practice sessions when I would do jumping jacks, nonstop, by the thousands, I discovered that fifteen minutes per thousand was the most efficient pace for my physique. If I went a little slower or a little faster, I would get tired sooner—because energy was being wasted by my jumping off-resonance, at a speed that wasn't ideal for my body.

This is the essence of tempo, and it's an important concept in pretty much all sport activities—pitching or hitting a baseball, shooting a basketball, running, swimming, etc. So one of the things you need to work on during your golf-swing practice is finding the ideal tempo, which will be specific to your body and the club you have in your hands at the time.

In case you're wondering, my approximate 9,000 jumping jacks, executed over a two-hour-fifteen-minute session, fell just short of the record books.

Your body type and the state of your body at the time (hungry, sated, tired, rested, etc.) will determine your ideal tempo during any particular swing attempt. The table below presents a set of body-type/swing-speed combinations that should work out as good general approximations for people of average size. The time for the swing is stated in seconds, measured from initial take-back of the club to ball impact. There will also be a slight variance in the ideal tempo depending on which club you are using. For example, the best driver tempo might be a little slower than the best pitching-wedge tempo.

Body Type	Swing Speed (sec)
Short	2.0 to 2.5
Medium	2.5 to 2.75
Tall	2.75 to 3.0

While the timing of the swing is the central part of your tempo, the complete or total tempo includes those moments leading up to initiating the backswing. The visioning and set-up time, including the total of your pre-shot routine, along with that swing frequency, all combine to establish your overall tempo.

Tempo is an important concept in your marriage relationship, too. The correct tempo creates more comfort for your partner as the need to resolve issues of communication or other misunderstandings comes up. When communicating with your spouse during trouble times, you want to have minimum deflection of incoming energy from him or her, and maximum acceptance of outgoing energy from you. This is marriage resonance, and it can only happen if you have the correct tempo for the relationship.

There is no handy matrix of clock times you can relate to an ideal tempo for your marriage, because physical clock time doesn't translate directly to marriage-relationship clock time.

The body-type equivalent of your intimate-partner relationship comes from your communication styles, problem-solving history, unresolved conflicts hanging out there in the relationship, your pre-shout routine habit, etc. Think about what it is you desire from your partner in terms of his or her response, verbal or otherwise. Try to sense how comfortable or uncomfortable she or he is with the style and sense of urgency with which you like to take care of things.

Problem solving in your marriage is like a dance. If your movements aren't synchronized, you step on each other's toes. The ideal tempo will be one where you can both work things out comfortably because you have an acceptable combined sense of urgency around that issue and are completely comfortable telling the other exactly how you feel about it. If he or she isn't ready to be receptive to the nature of the energy you're about to put out, you're going to be off tempo and may have to leave the house for a while.

Men's vs. Women's Diaries

Wife's Diary:

Tonight I thought my husband was acting weird. We'd made plans to meet at a nice restaurant for dinner. I was shopping with my friends all day long, so I thought he was upset at the fact that I was a bit late, but he made no comment on it. Conversation wasn't flowing, so I suggested that we go somewhere quiet so we could talk. He agreed, but he didn't say much.

I asked him what was wrong. He said, "Nothing." I asked him if it was my fault that he was upset. He said he wasn't upset, that it had nothing to do with me and not to worry about it. On the way home, I told him that I loved him. He smiled slightly and kept driving. I can't explain his behavior. I don't know why he didn't say, "I love you, too."

When we got home, I felt as if I'd lost him completely and he wanted nothing to do with me anymore. He just sat there quietly and watched TV. He continued to seem distant and absent. Finally, with silence all around us, I decided to go to bed. About fifteen minutes later, he came to bed. But I still felt that he was distracted and that his thoughts were somewhere else. He fell asleep. I cried. I don't know what to do. I'm almost sure that his thoughts are with someone else. My life is a disaster.

Husband's Diary:

A two-foot putt. Who the hell misses a two-foot putt?

Chapter 12

You Want Control? Why?

Within your heart lies the secret of life,
joy and sorrow, pressure and strife...
love is all of these things.
—The Temptations (from *The Prophet*)

Rather than trying to force it or press the issue,
I'm going to be patient.
—Phil Mickelson (during a year-long slump)

In golf, you work hard to develop a swing you believe you can control.

In marriage, you must learn to be okay with your life feeling like it's out of control.

After the honeymoon, you must learn to be okay with your life feeling like it's out of control, because in many respects it is, and in some ways that can be seen as good news. It's good news if you learn to ride with it. It's not good news if all you can think is, *Why does my life feel like it's out of control?*

Once, when asked what style he practiced, the late, great, martial-arts expert Bruce Lee calmly said, "I practice the art of fighting without fighting." Fighting without fighting means being in control—by not letting the desire to be in control get in the way.

If you can hold a state of mind that is relaxed, positive, and intensely purposeful in the face of some perceived threat to your physical, mental, or emotional well-being, you are fighting without fighting.

This concept is helpful regardless of whether you seek to be a top martial artist, golf or other sports competitor, business professional, IT engineer, or anything else involving a competitive dimension. It's also a very important skill when it comes to being a successful spouse.

A major challenge to golfers at all levels is learning how to let go of that bogey, double bogey, or dreaded "other" you just scored on the previous hole. Some unfortunate players, after a disastrous hole, spend the next three holes bemoaning and reliving that one bad experience! You can imagine what that does for those next three holes.

In marriage, you must learn to put an unfortunate event in the past and, after you've learned from it—leave it there! In golf, you pretty much know what you did wrong immediately afterward. In fact, it's amazing how obvious the reason for the mistake can be—after the fact. Sure, take a few minutes to understand what happened and make any needed adjustments, but after that you must put it away and let it go—because if you don't, it will take you to a place of negative energy and tension.

It's understandable that when you play golf, you want to see how well you can score (if you're in a tournament, you want to win, and to win you have to score well), but too much focus on that score can become its own source of tension and distraction.

I discovered years ago, in my own golf game, that if I'm having a good round and at, say, the seventeenth tee I start thinking about what I need to do on the next two holes to break eighty or break par or achieve a personal best, I'll very likely play my worst two holes of the round.

Many touring professional golfers, if they're at or near the top of the leaderboard on Sunday, will try to avoid looking at the scoreboard. They certainly hear the roar of the crowd if someone sinks a birdie putt or flags an approach, but that's not as distracting as actually seeing the score and noticing that a competitor just tied or passed you. Actually seeing it makes it harder for you to center the next time you're standing over the ball, because now you know you "need" birdie on this hole— which is the wrong thing to be thinking when you're trying to relax over a shot. There's nothing wrong with being aware of the score, as long as you can keep it from getting in the way of your focus.

In marriage, you want the kind of control that comes without fighting for it. Making control an end in itself causes you to focus on such negatives as fear, which inhibits your ability to center and relax. If we can step away from that fight-with-fear and that need to exert control, we can then relax enough to actually have more control—first over ourselves, then over the situation.

Chilling out in your relationship has a lot to do with giving up on keeping score, or the sting of unfortunate past events, or the need to always be right. Keeping score in your marriage happens during an argument or problem situation where you remind your wife or husband of that time he or she did something that was hurtful, brought hardship to the family, or was, in your mind, just plain stupid.

This negative 'Remember when?' statement only serves to distract you from what's in front of you right now and makes it more difficult to find a positive resolution. Your aim should be to ensure that you're handling problems in your relationship in ways that make the relationship stronger and more directed toward your intent. Keeping your spouse's screw-ups fresh and at the front of your memory will work against that objective and is more about your ego than anything else.

The relationship grows when you can keep the bad memories in the past and away from current challenges. If you keep bringing those negative statements about past problems into the conversation, you build up an energy that starts to work against empathy and good communications—and this will push your relationship in a direction that works against your intent.

Sometimes you're angered by the things your spouse says or does because those things make you afraid. The fear is there because you internalize what he or she said or did as a signal that the relationship is going in an uncontrollable direction. But while it may be true that the relationship is changing direction and moving away from where you want it to go, really all that means is that you both have some work to do in adjusting things. Whatever the situation, reacting out of fear will usually make it worse.

It is said that *un*learning is the beginning of learning. All relationships draw you into the occasional battle. It is important to fight these battles, but we must learn to do so while focusing beyond the competition (with our partners and ourselves)—in other words, we must learn to fight without fighting. You need to be fully engaged in your marriage when problems arise and work through those problems with a full measure of positive energy and relaxed focus. Negative emotions happen because they're part of human nature. We have to learn to take that energy, process it, and have it produce something positive. If negative emotions go unprocessed, they will dictate our attitudes in ways that lead to even greater problems.

Jesper Parnevik's trying "harder and harder" meant that he was fighting his golf swing more and more. Fighting your swing— or fighting that challenging marriage situation—is exactly the opposite of what you want to do. *Don't fight it, invite it.*

By "invite it" I mean to welcome the physical sensation that comes with the fear, as a trigger for relaxation. Get to know what that initial urge to fight feels like, before you habitually respond to something you don't like. Familiarizing yourself with that physical sensation will help you check out of the negative emotion and move on to a place where you can fully commit to an acceptable action.

For your marriage, that acceptable action would be communicating how you feel and starting a dialogue about the question or issue. For golf, the acceptable action would be the smooth takeaway of the club, followed by a smooth transition from backswing to forward-swing.

Many golfers who perceive a threat to their emotional security (e.g., a looming water hazard) allow fear to build to the point where it severely distorts the way in which the mind and body relate to each other. Often the effect this has on their swing is both apparent and dramatic. The swing tempo changes, the swing plane distorts, the club transition becomes erratic—all resulting in a total breakdown of the golf-swing relationship for a critical two or three seconds. One can avoid this fate by becoming so intimately familiar with that initial sensation that it's possible to be relaxed when feeling it. When that happens, the fear just goes away.

I knew a guy who had a big problem with shanking (hitting the ball perpendicular to where it should be going) his short irons. Believe it or not, I've seen Hall of Fame golfers do the same thing, and it can really get into a golfer's head—at any level. When I asked my friend what was happening, he said he just couldn't figure it out. As he explained it, he'd be standing over, say, a pitching wedge, and thinking to himself, "Just don't shank it." And, sure enough, he'd get the toe of the club stuck or open the face while trying to steer it, and off to the right it would go. Which makes for a nice paraphrase of Descartes: "I think, therefore I shank." I'm sure some work on swing mechanics would help, but his problem had just as much to do with what was going on in his head. It's not so much the act of thinking that causes the problem; it's what you're thinking and when you think it.

I recall one of my own 'Tin Cup' moments when my teenage son and I were out playing and came to an intimidating par three that was all carry, over water. My son stepped up and promptly put his tee shot in the water. I listened to him growl and vent for a few moments before trying to help him settle down. I suggested he take a few seconds to visualize the water as grass, thinking that might help him relax. His next shot arced beautifully with a slight draw and landed pretty much in the middle of the green.

I then stepped up to the tee and immediately noticed I couldn't get comfortable over the ball. There was a kind of optical strangeness with the angle of the tee box and the direction of the green that kept me doubting my setup. I stepped back for a moment and took a couple of deep breaths but still couldn't seem to get centered and fully committed to the shot. I took the swing anyway. The first ball went in the water, as did the second. After that, I broke out in laughter and thought about the irony of the situation, considering the advice I'd just given my son. The laughter was just what I needed, because it allowed me to relax and get rid of my tension. My third shot was a beauty, right to the center of the green and inside my son's position.

From time to time, we all experience brief periods of illusion where we think we're in control. This gives rise to expectations that are not met by reality—and we declare things to be out of control, whereupon we start looking for ways to ease our pain and suffering. Too often we seek to accomplish this by running from our marriage or quitting golf. Don't give up—just learn to laugh a little, and look forward to the next opportunity to do it again.

Chapter 13

Torsion Not Tension

From an evolutionary perspective,
love itself exists to meet the needs of the neocortex.
If we didn't have a neocortex,
then lust would be quite sufficient to guarantee reproduction.
—Ray Kurzweil

If a lot of people gripped a knife and fork
the way they do a golf club,
they'd starve to death.
—Sam Snead

Torsion comes from coiling your body; tension comes from coiling your mind.

Torsion comes from coiling your body and creating a potential energy store that is released when you uncoil, much like twisting a rubber band or ribbon segment then releasing it. The ribbon could be made of rubber, metal, wood, plastic, or just about any other material. The principle is the same. Only the torsion characteristics differ, as is the case with different golfers, owing to different body types and conditions. The body is rotated and the club taken back to momentarily store up the maximum amount of potential energy (via torsion) without becoming unstable, or losing your balance or causing you to become tense. Tension will happen if you go too far, or sense discomfort and let your body communicate that to your mind, or vice versa. When that tension enters into the swing process, it creates such problems as lack of commitment, lack of trust, etc. The body creates torsion, the mind creates the tension. We want maximum torsion without tension.

The physical power for the golf swing comes primarily from the lower body. (Many believe the lower body to be the source of power in marriage, too.) Knowing how to use the legs and hips, especially at the start of the uncoiling motion, is a key for proper club release. This same hip-whip principle is also important for delivering energy in many other sports, such as martial arts, boxing, tennis, baseball, football, etc.

In marriage, torsion can be represented by the potential energy of interaction that you and your spouse have built up while trying to work things out when you have differing opinions or views. The total torsion energy is the sum of the difference that exists between your viewpoints as it relates to the various ways you might go about solving a problem. It's like twisting that rubber ribbon. The challenge is to release that potential energy in a way that propels your marriage in the direction of your intent. Tension (fear, anger, and blame) will drain the energy away from that direction. The energy (torsion and tension) might be at a high level when you have different views about raising kids, and at a lower level when you're trying to agree on how much salt to use in the chicken broth.

Just as it is with your golf-swing relationship, getting the tension out of your marriage relationship will help you to achieve a high level of trust, commitment, follow-through, etc. There are many techniques that can be effective for reducing tension in your marriage. A few examples would be agreeing to take a time out, having a pillow fight (or other playful activity), making love, etc.

Guys often believe that when tension builds up, they need to take the situation by the horns and do something forceful and definitive to get things under control. In both golf and marriage we're advised to be cautious when picking those opportunities to be aggressive. Trying to force something to happen has a way of costing you more in both golf-swing and marital relationships. Your golfing buddies might be happy to give you a mulligan, but your wife may not.

Be sure to remain emotionally available when things get tense. Find the tension-cutting techniques that work best for the two of you, and practice using them even when things aren't so tense. The usual cause of tension is fear on the part of one or both partners. If you make a habit of doing something that takes your mind away from that fear, it will help you cut the tension.

Marriage "Yips"

The late, great, Scottish golfer Tommy Armour, who was a major force on the pro circuit in the early part of the twentieth century, might be confused by the phrase "curing the yips." Mr. Armour, who himself popularized the term "yips," believed there was nothing to be done about this condition, and the yips ultimately led to his exit from competitive golf.

The yips are a well-known golfing malady which is thought to affect more than forty percent of male golfers and an apparently smaller percentage of female golfers. As it turns out, the more experienced the golfer, the more likely he or she will be to have the yips. The term is used to describe involuntary movements and loss of motor function that happens for no outwardly apparent reason. The condition is characterized by jerky, spasmodic twitches or a freezing up and occurs most noticeably when the golfer is standing over a putt.

The yips are thought to be caused by a neurologic dysfunction due to neurons misfiring in the motor-sensory cortex and the thin layer of neural tissue (basal ganglia) covering the brain. The stress and tension preceding the intended movement affect the chemistry of the brain. This causes the muscle group the brain commands to contract in a way that is not well coordinated with adjacent muscles, which need to relax in order to permit a smooth and controlled motion (putting stroke, full or partial swing, etc.). Oxygen deprivation from arrested breathing caused by tension and fear may also contribute to this condition.

Popular techniques used to combat the yips include changing equipment (some golfers use longer putters to minimize emphasis on the wrist muscles) and various stress-management techniques. Certain over-the-counter drugs have also been known to give some relief. Some golfers even try alcohol to help settle their nerves before a competitive round—an approach that generally tends to do more harm than good in the long run.

And it's not just golfers or other athletes who get the yips. The condition is known to be a problem for many musicians, chefs, writers, and other professionals whose activities require long-term fine-motor repetition.

You can get the yips in your marriage, too. In that case, the yips happen when you develop a tendency to mentally check out or become instantaneously irritated before your spouse finishes what he or she has to say. This can happen because you have been conditioned toward the negative and assume there's no way that whatever the other person's about to say is going to make you feel happy.

As with golf yips, marriage yips also come with a randomized and involuntary firing of neurons, which may keep you from processing your spouse's words in an orderly fashion. In fact, it can even prevent you from having any idea of what she or he just said or how you should best respond. This can provoke a kind of default fight-or-flight response that causes you to say something or do something unfortunate—which then leads to his or her next statement being even more incomprehensible.

A good way to combat the marriage yips is to employ such stress-management techniques as meditation or eating high-cocoa chocolate. One approach I would personally suggest is simply trying to anticipate that something good (that is, useful for moving the situation forward) will come from your spouse's remarks. Even if the words that come out of his or her mouth hit your ears and trigger a defensive emotional stance, try to fully focus, while using your relaxation technique, on finding something positive in the other's view or perception. Anticipate that, and be ready to add something constructive to the remark.

Lamaze Class

The room was full of pregnant women and their partners, and the Lamaze class was in full swing. The instructor was teaching the women to breathe properly, along with informing the men how to give the necessary assurances at this stage of the plan. The teacher then announced, "Ladies, exercise is GOOD for you! Walking is especially beneficial. And gentlemen, it wouldn't hurt YOU to take the time to go walking with your partner!"

The room became very quiet. Finally, a man in the middle of the group raised his hand.

"Yes?" the teacher said.

The man said, "Is it all right if she carries a golf bag while we walk?"

Chapter 14

Trust or Bust

Golf is a hard game to figure.
One day you will go out and slice it, shank it, hit into all the traps
and miss every green.
The next day you go out and, for no reason at all, you really stink.
—Bob Hope

Commitment means
staying loyal to what you said you were going to do
long after the mood you said it in has left you.
—Orebela Gbenga

Commit to and trust your swing in golf. Commit to and trust your intent in marriage.

Being committed allows you to relax and settle enough to respond positively to any challenge that comes up. This ability is necessary if you intend to honestly attempt to make your marriage work over the long term. Commitment is also required if you want to consistently strike a golf ball well. Both golf and marriage involve multiple levels of commitment.

We often hear about the importance of having a "commitment to excellence." In golf and marriage, excellence is a by-product of understanding your intent and being fully committed to it. When you're committed, you're all in on the effort that lies before you, in terms of your overall development as well as the smaller challenges that make up the larger effort. If you're fully committed to your relationship, you won't be looking for potential escape routes when the going gets tough. Likewise, you won't hear that tiny voice in the back of your mind asking whether or not you really want to stick with this. Being fully committed means accepting the responsibility that comes with being determined to succeed.

For golf, you must commit to traveling to the driving range and getting out on the course. You must also commit each time you find yourself standing over the ball, contemplating a shot. Your level of commitment at that moment will determine how well you execute the golf swing. This is true in both simple and difficult golf-shot situations.

Your golf swing "knows" whether or not you're fully committed. Golf-swing commitment starts with visualizing the flight of the ball and believing that you really have that shot in your bag. Maybe you just want to have fun with the situation or show off a bit and decide you're going to hit a 250-yard punch-cut fade under a low-hanging tree limb, over water, and onto a relatively small green—because you need birdie to win the match. Unless you're an elite touring pro, chances are you won't be able to fully commit to that swing, because it's probably a shot you've never made and never practiced.

The fear that your mind communicates to your body will stymie full commitment and very likely add two or three strokes to your score. If you're really serious about getting the best result in this situation, you might instead decide to lay up a short iron back from the water's edge, then try to get a wedge close enough to one-putt for that birdie. It's easier to commit to these swings than to expect the unlikely one-shot miracle. This, in turn, makes success more likely.

I took a small and informal poll of married friends and acquaintances, asking them to list the things they thought were key to a successful marriage. Every female respondent placed commitment on the list, in most cases at or near the top. The male respondents were for the most part confused by the question and asked me for the answer.

Without commitment, married people tend to cut and run at the first sign of trouble. Even if they don't take physical flight, they'll often check out mentally and emotionally when difficult times come. This reduces or destroys their ability to work through the problem.

Your spouse can see or sense your lack of commitment in the way you communicate and respond during routine interactions. If your spouse comes to believe that you're not committed, he or she will (consciously or subconsciously) seek ways to make changes in the relationship—changes that (hopefully) shore up his or her sense of emotional security. Usually this effort takes the form of wanting the other person to do or be something different. This may be okay if your spouse happens to have a strong sense of self, good communication skills, emotional maturity, and confidence—in which case he or she may go along with your wishes in the name of helping you to become more committed to the relationship. On the other hand, if your spouse is not strong, or not so solid or capable in terms of emotional security and people skills, the shakiness he or she feels coming from you will tend to be amplified—resulting in a crisis, a gradual demise of the relationship, or both.

If your original intent doesn't fully commit you to the relationship, you probably shouldn't be there in the first place. However, if you believe that you started out committed, and for some reason that changed or is changing, it's a good idea to revisit your intent and try to find clarity about the mission(s) associated with that intent. In both golf and marriage, commitment to the relationship ultimately equates to commitment to your intent.

Marriage and family workshops are ubiquitous in communities throughout the country and usually include discussions about something called *conditional commitment.* This term describes a situation where you're committed to the relationship, but only so long as things are going well and the emotional challenge level is low. With conditional commitment, the tendency is to blame the other person when tough problems arise. When you put the blame on your spouse, you imply that he or she needs a change of attitude or way of being. When your partner pushes back on that, the two of you tend to drift apart. True commitment means not fearing the difficult times, because dealing with them successfully creates progress toward maturing the relationship and fulfilling your intent.

Patience works hand in hand with commitment. The more committed you are, the more patient you'll be. Patience is of critical importance, because you must learn to deal with change, and that may take considerable time and energy. Remember, your partner is also dealing with the relationship issue of the moment and may not see or understand it in the same way you do. Men and women define and solve problems differently.

In golf, you must be patient with swing-development issues and with the inevitable adjustments that changes in your mind and body will require over time. Such adjustments may—depending on the individual—be ongoing, or they may be brief and intense.

Trust and commitment are like two sides of the same coin. If you don't trust the other person, you won't commit fully to a relationship with him or her. It's the same with golf. If you don't (for whatever reason) trust your swing to be ready to advance the ball, there's no way you'll be fully committed to that swing.

A rational person wouldn't marry someone he or she didn't trust, unless their intent had to do with achieving some desperate end such as social acceptance (e.g., getting a green card), getting out of some kind of trouble, monetary gain, personal safety or survival, etc. In such a case, the only trust needed is that the person he or she is marrying can deliver the conditions required to achieve those ends. Such marriages are referred to as marriages of convenience, and they generally come crashing down once the need or crisis has been met or resolved, or when it becomes clear that the marriage will fail to deliver on that front.

In the best cases, most people try to understand their betrothed's intent and reason for wanting to get married, then decide how trustworthy the person is based on that understanding and the history of the relationship. Indeed, your prospective bride or groom can have the best of intentions and yet be untrustworthy, simply because she or he lacks the skills needed to hold up his or her end of the bargain. They may, for example, lack the maturity to handle the rigors of marriage, or lack the experience to make good family-oriented decisions.

If you're aware of this situation at the start, you might choose to go ahead anyway, placing your trust in your own ability to compensate for your partner's shortcomings. Pursuing this course can be either very heroic or very stupid. In either case, it probably requires that you adjust your initial expectations. A better decision might be to hold off—for now—on getting married.

Living with someone you don't trust guarantees a hellish life, unless you're able to deal with a situation that always has you second-guessing what she really means, or what he's really up to. In the end, you'll never feel settled in a marriage without trust. You will not communicate well with each other or feel secure in the relationship, and you'll look for ways to put the blame on your spouse at every turn.

I recall hearing a guy describe the way in which his criteria for the ideal bride had evolved over time. He said that he used to have a long list of qualities this woman would need to possess—such things as physical beauty (he wanted a 9 or a 10), athletic prowess, high intellect, and so on. Now, he hopes to find someone with just three characteristics:

1. Someone he can get along with most of the time.

2. A good mother for their children.

3. Someone he can trust to help make wise family decisions.

What if you trusted someone who then made a mistake that called that trust into question? This is where the ability to communicate with each other is tested. The two of you need to decide what it will take to restore that trust, because if you can't get the trust back, you can probably kiss the relationship goodbye.

In golf, you must trust your golf swing to deliver on the desired ball-strike. Otherwise you're setting yourself up for a bad experience on that hole. Once you've addressed the ball and are ready to begin your backswing, even one iota of creeping doubt (causing you to question the swing's outcome) can result in de-centering and swing distortion. Generally speaking, you develop trust in your golf swing by building confidence in your ability to execute it correctly and repeatedly. This is where hours and hours of practice make their mark.

Most professional golfers say you shouldn't try a shot on the course unless you've practiced beforehand. Without that practice, you won't have the requisite confidence in your ability to pull off the shot. The trust you need won't be there during those critical few seconds that start when you take the club back, and continue through the critical transition from backswing to forward-swing. This lack of trust will invariably cause you to attempt a change while you're in midswing—for example, trying to steer the ball instead of letting the impact happen as effortlessly as it needs to. Your swing will respond to this lack of trust by introducing ball-impact error.

In marriage, lack of confidence in your partner's ability and desire to do the right thing leads to lack of trust. That and the presence of fear exist in direct proportion to each other. In fact, fear is generally at the base of any unwillingness to trust. We know what fear does to the relationship with your golf swing. It will have the same effect on the relationship with your intimate partner. You build confidence and trust in your relationship by getting to know your partner through activities and conversations, and by remaining present to work through family problems together.

Fast Learner

Two women were talking the other day over tea. "Did I tell you that my husband has taken up golf?" the first lady asked her friend.

"No, as a matter of fact, you didn't," her friend replied. "How's he doing?"

"Evidently, very well," said the first woman. "He's only played three times, but his friends tell me that he's already throwing his clubs as far as men who've been playing the game for years!"

Chapter 15

What's Love Got to Do With It?

We learn so many things from golf—how to suffer, for instance.
—Bruce Lansky

*Be faithful in small things
because it is in them that your strength lies.*
—Mother Teresa

Your marriage needs love and chocolates, as does your golf swing.

Love is merciless but essential. Merciless, because it makes you take crazy risks. Essential because without crazy risks, we'll never get to where we want to go.

As it turns out, love is the key ingredient for a successful marriage and for a successful golf swing. Love is the most oft-cited reason people give for getting married. Love is also the reason people seem to have such a hard time understanding and dealing with a romantic relationship.

But what the heck is love, anyway? I certainly love it when (all too infrequently) I get a tap-in birdie on the golf course. But is that really love? If so, it's only one of many different kinds of love. We love our children, probably in a way we could never love anyone or anything else. You may love your work, your hobbies, your country, your favorite sports team, etc., yet none of these is the same as the love you feel when you're *in love* with another person. Being in love means being totally vulnerable and in a state of what I would call happy confusion.

One problem with romantic love is that we're never really sure of what we're feeling, why we feel it, or what it's actually made of (which is part of what makes love so fascinating). We just know that, at this time, this particular person makes us feel like we're in love, and we're therefore ready to accept whatever risks may be associated with embracing that love, nurturing it, and trying like hell to make it last.

Love is probably the most powerful motivation for people to marry, because it transcends rational judgment. Indeed, if more people gave rational judgment priority over love, there would be considerably fewer marriages and divorces. It's that thing we call love that makes most marriages the wild, fascinating, frustrating adventures they become. Choosing to marry for love means choosing to put yourself in a place where you're certain to experience intense feelings you've never dealt with before.

When you're in love, you eventually realize that you'll experience periods of self-doubt and confusion about your life's purpose. Feeling that way with your golf swing compares favorably to feeling that way with your marriage. With your golf swing, it's easier to believe that the relationship will improve as your understanding of who you are improves. In marriage, improvement takes longer, because marriage almost always encourages more confusion about who you are. However, by learning to be more appreciative of the love you have for your golf swing, you will naturally develop better skills for appreciating the love you have for your spouse.

How much in love you are matters too, but in slightly different ways for golf and marriage. In marriage, the greater the magnitude of your love, the more intense will be the feeling of confusion when things don't go according to plan. This causes a higher level of fear about your future and more questions about the meaning of your life. On the other hand, a more intense love for your golf swing will draw you closer to it during adversity, increasing your excitement about possible solutions to the problem. If you remain aware, the same excitement can be there for resolving the marriage problem.

There is *being in love*, and there's *making love*. As you would expect, the more in love you are, the better at making love you can be.

Make Love to Your Golf Swing

Anything you can have an intimate relationship with, you can make love to, so to speak, including your golf swing.

When we speak of making love to another person, we understand that both physical and nonphysical components are involved. With your golf swing, the physical part is centered on the style and nature of the grip you're using and the way you've trained yourself to swing that particular club. The nonphysical part is essentially the same as it is with your wife, husband, or whomever.

The essence of making love to another person lies in the desire and ability to think of and feel them as you. To the extent that you can do this—think of them as yourself—you'll gain an innate sense of how to generate great satisfaction and project a feeling of oneness through your touch.

It's the same with making love to your golf swing. The grip you use with the club is so important because the grip sets the physical stage for your golf-swing relationship. Too tight is uncomfortable and builds tension, too loose fails to transmit energy and commitment correctly. Your grip is the interface between your total instantaneous being and your swing action. It allows your golf swing to become—you. In this way, in both cases (making love to your spouse and making love to your golf swing) you are, essentially, making love to yourself.

> *The [golf] grip ... is man's connection to the world outside himself.*
>
> *The hands ... are where the subjective meets the objective. Where we "in here" meet the world "out there." True intelligence ... does not reside in the brain, but in the hands.*
> —Bagger Vance

Making love to your spouse (not just having sex) is an important opportunity for you to communicate, nonverbally, your commitment to the relationship. Making wholesome love helps to push out both physiological and psychological tensions and helps keep both partners open to an increased understanding of the other's individual nature, as well as the nature of the relationship itself.

Similarly, when you make love to your golf swing, you're helping your relationship to become a more natural thing. This can reach the point where, when you grasp the club, you can feel yourself become something more than you were prior to holding it (just as you can when passionately embracing your spouse). This is the essence of making love in both marriage and golf: You become better in ways that help you overcome short-term challenges. You're actually nourishing your ability to serve your greater intent.

Dear Abby,

I've never written to you before, but I really need your advice. I have suspected for some time now that my wife has been cheating on me. The usual signs: the phone rings but if I answer, the caller hangs up. My wife has been going out with "the girls" a lot recently, although when I ask their names she always says, "Just some friends from work, you don't know them." I always try to stay awake to look out for her coming home, but I usually fall asleep. Anyway, I have never approached the subject with my wife. I think deep down I just didn't want to know the truth, but last night she went out again and I decided to really check on her.

Around midnight, I decided to hide in the garage behind my golf clubs so I could get a good view of the whole street when she arrived home from a night out with "the girls." It was at that moment, crouching behind my clubs, that I noticed that the graphite shaft on my driver appeared to have a hairline crack right by the club head. Is this something I can fix myself or should I take it back to the pro shop where I bought it?

Chapter 16

O Say Can You See?

When a girl marries, she exchanges the attentions of many men for the inattention of just one.
—Helen Rowland

Golf is horrifying, humiliating, and humbling, but I can't wait to do it again.
—Unknown

In golf and in marriage, communication is key to solving problems. Learn to be sensitive to what might seem like very strange feedback.

Being sensitive to feedback means paying attention, and being mindful of what's coming back after you've sent your message.

Competitive golf is played mainly on a five-and-a-half-inch course—the space between your ears.
—Bobby Jones

The space between your ears, as Mr. Jones calls it, not only determines what you decide to do with what comes your way, but indeed whether or not you even know something was sent your way—like the subtle and complex statement your spouse made at the dinner table. Perhaps you weren't quite sure what was meant and decided not to press for clarity in the hope that you could finish eating and get out the door. Or maybe something like the tiny vibration you felt in your right hand but not in your left after making a golf swing that sent the ball well right of the green. That's important feedback. Don't ignore it.

The space between your ears is where the mental, physical, and emotional parts converge to handle all the incoming and outgoing communications you will ever have. One proven approach in helping to develop this communication ability is the practice of meditation. That's right—meditation. One style that's becoming more popular these days is known as mindfulness meditation.

Mindfulness meditation has found its way into such institutions as schools, health centers, and corporations, as well as private homes, in the United States and elsewhere. In mindfulness meditation, you simultaneously concentrate on some bodily sensation such as your breath or heartbeat while also remaining mindful of what's going on around you.

This dual-awareness training can help you manage the sensations that take place inside you before you communicate to the outside world. This, in turn, improves your ability to come up with a response that won't land you in a golf hazard or divorce court. Being able to recognize and feel what's happening with you is the step that takes place just before you process outside stimuli and respond to it, on the golf course or at home.

Mindfulness-meditation practice can help fend off one of modern society's greatest afflictions—the high-stress lifestyle. Even corporations are getting into the act, with many now touting this kind of training and its ability to help the bottom line.

Being mindful while you meditate teaches you to experience your environment in the way most wives and husbands would like their spouse to experience it—nonjudgmentally. It helps you to be more aware of your own sensations, as well as of things in your immediate vicinity (for example, what feelings your partner might be experiencing at that moment). Mastering this technique, you can learn to "sense the grasshopper at your feet"—a metaphor for the build up that happens before your spouse screams at you about not hearing what he or she just said. On the golf course, it's your swing that's screaming (through your golf club) to be heard. If you're mindful—really mindful—you'll hear it clearly.

The ancient Tibetan word for meditation, *Gom*, means to become familiar with oneself. Meditation has a history stretching back several thousand years and is practiced the world over in dozens of different schools, styles, and forms. There are guided and unguided meditation practices, meditation styles that use sounds and mantras, and those that require the practitioner to sit in silent contemplation. Style doesn't matter. Any meditation practice, done with regularity and focus, will help you relax, help you get to know the sensations that cause you to react, and help you make decisions based on your intent rather than your fears. My wife and I used to meditate together. Now we mediate separately, but the practice continues to help us with our relationship.

Yoga is a popular and ancient form of dynamic meditation. With yoga, you get multiple benefits, because you work on developing greater physical strength and flexibility (a key for golf) while simultaneously improving mental calmness and relaxed focus. Many of the well-known, winning, professional golfers are yoga practitioners.

Golf can also be thought of as a form of dynamic meditation. The same principles of mind-body connectivity you apply in developing your meditation or yoga practice also apply as you develop the relationship with your golf swing. Quiet focus is key to relaxing and allowing yourself to feel what's going on with your swing. The more you do this, the more similar golf and yoga will feel, improving your ability to focus and center over any shot.

Becoming more mindful of what your body goes through while you execute the golf swing helps you improve your swing execution, resulting in an improved relationship with it. Being with your wife or husband will never feel exactly like yoga, but the ability to stay focused while twisting your body is a skill that can add happiness to your marriage.

If you add a meditation practice (dynamic or otherwise) to your daily routine, you'll become more proficient at being with your feelings during the critical seconds immediately following a dust-up with your spouse. Meditation practice will help you get to know *you*, which will help build the habit of checking in with what you feel before you act. This will help correct the tendency to react (as many do) in an angry or frustrated manner.

In recent years, scientists all over the world have done a great deal of research seeking to understand whether, and how, meditation actually affects the physical brain. Neuropsychologists have long understood there to be a kind of plasticity in the part of the brain that deals with social interactions. In other words, we're not completely hard-wired when it comes to those soft skills we might work on during a behavior-therapy session.

The results of this research are in, and the data confirm that the more you meditate, the more your brain changes for the better. With meditation, your brain changes in such a way that, in most situations, you find it easier to relax and remain calm. Meditation-induced brain changes cause you to be more compassionate, empathic, and understanding (your spouse will like that!), and enhances your ability to focus and see things clearly.

This, in turn, makes you better able to deal with those heat-of-the-moment situations where you get emotionally fired up and tend say or do things you'll regret soon after. In marriage, those heat-of-the-moment situations may come up fairly regularly. In golf, just about every attempt to advance the ball can be a heat-of-the-moment equivalent.

And there's no need to meditate for hours at a time. Just twenty minutes a day devoted to the practice will make a difference in how your brain and mind work. The key is making it part of your daily routine, until it becomes a habit.

Chapter 17

Simple Not Simpleton

But give me a lousy swing
and the ability to win under pressure any day
over a swing that looks good but doesn't get the job done.
—Gary Player

There are two types of women, all right? There's type A and type B.
Type A, they're real easy – they jump right into bed with you boom,
boom, boom. Then later on they break your balls. Then there's type
B ... you gotta wine them ... dine them. Then later on ...
they break your balls.
—from *Jersey Boys*, directed by Clint Eastwood

A simple golf swing will help lower your score. A simple marriage relationship will help eliminate the need for a score.

One of the reasons the golf swing is such a challenge is that so many different parts of your body (plus your mind and emotions) can be trying to move simultaneously, in directions that are not entirely compatible. This creates a very complex motion in space-time. Your practice should be designed to simplify that motion, with as few things as possible moving independently.

Visualize all these different parts as connected with hinges or axes of movement (your mind and emotions are hinged to your body through life experiences). The challenge, when addressing a golf shot, is to ensure that as many of these hinges as possible move in the desired direction during that brief time of execution. When the motion of these parts is coordinated, energy is efficiently and smoothly transmitted, and the swing becomes a single motion of your entire self (mind, body, and spirit) as you exist in that moment.

A good way to work on developing simplicity during your golf-swing practice is to remind yourself that your entire body takes part in the swing. When starting out, you'll focus on arms, hips, shoulders, head, etc., as individual components of the swing. But as soon as you can, begin thinking of it as one continuous motion. If you can get your swing to feel like a single action, it will give you maximum repeatability with maximum energy transfer and greater durability.

Sometimes when watching a Tour event you'll hear the broadcast commentator remark about how a player's swing might have broken down under the pressure of a tough shot situation (especially if he has a one- or two-stroke lead on the back nine on Sunday). The more complex the swing, the more likely it is that breakdown will take place. This happens because the more complex the swing, the greater will be the distortion caused by small amounts of fear and doubt. Golf-swing simplicity will help keep such distortion to a minimum and allow the swing to hold up better under the pressures of difficult shot situations.

Marriage has more moving parts than golf.

Simplicity helps create a favorable environment in which to develop your relationships, by making it easier for you to focus on the deeper aspects of the actions you take. In golf, that means learning how to instantaneously center and execute each shot with greater depth, understanding, and flow. In marriage, it means pretty much the same thing—a deeper appreciation of the issue, a better ability to understand where your spouse is coming from, and a response more suited to your true intent.

In marriage, you decide which factors you will allow to enter into a problem situation. Other family members, difficulties at work, kids, old girl- or boyfriends, ex-husbands, money, sex, etc., can all become potential factors in a decision regarding any particular marital problem. In marriage, greater simplicity helps you and your partner avoid getting stuck, so you can get to the root of the problem more quickly.

Most models of an enlightened existence center around the idea of simplicity. When we study the well-known gurus, prophets, and holy people in human history, we find that they all tended to lead very simple lives. This is partly to keep distractions to a minimum (it's harder to focus on peace and love when you're worried about your Ferrari getting towed), and partly to help develop a greater appreciation for the fundamentals of existence.

In your marriage, keeping it simple helps your partner to see and understand where you're coming from, where you're going, and what needs you have. This keeps the guessing to a minimum and reduces the wasted energy and uncertainty over trust issues that so often plague relationships.

One way to keep things simple is to be clear about what you want—right now—and what you believe getting that means to the both of you. Keeping it simple means working at being in lockstep with your partner and moving in a direction that supports the intent you have for your relationship.

Strong relationships are built in the same way the pyramids were constructed: by first ensuring that the foundation blocks are broad, solid, and simple, with another structural layer on top of the foundation blocks, a third layer atop that, and so on. Simplicity helps ensure that the foundation is strong and tight, giving the pyramid the ability to withstand forces that might otherwise upset or destroy it. The robustness and size of the foundation ultimately determine how high the pyramid can be. If your relationship enjoys a strong and simple foundation, your ability to handle ever higher levels of challenge will be greater.

Simplicity in your relationship improves when, for example, you can communicate with each other quickly, easily, and with good understanding. Simplicity is enhanced when you and your partner are in agreement on the basic requirements for quality in your relationship. This makes it easier for you to agree on an appropriate course of action when a problem arises.

Having to go back and rehash old issues each time a problem comes up is like thinking about what your feet are going to do every time you swing a golf club. Simplicity is there when the two of you are comfortable addressing a problem together and the health of your relationship depends on it. Keep it simple, and let the basic foundation of serving your intent dictate your actions.

Can You Do This?

After thirty-five years of marriage, a husband and wife went in for counseling. When asked what the problem was, the wife went into a tirade listing every problem they'd ever had in all the years they'd been married. On and on and on it went: neglect, lack of intimacy, emptiness, loneliness, feeling unloved and unlovable, an entire laundry list of unmet needs she'd endured.

Finally, after allowing this for a sufficient length of time, the therapist got up, walked around the desk, and asked the wife to stand. He then embraced and kissed her long and passion-

ately, as her husband watched with a raised eyebrow. The woman shut up and quietly sat down in a daze.

The therapist turned to the husband and said, "This is what your wife needs at least three times a week. Can you do this?"

To which the husband replied, "Well, I can drop her off here on Mondays and Wednesdays, but I play golf on Fridays."

Chapter 18

Relationship Trouble
Is Infinite

A finite game is played for the purpose of winning,
an infinite game for the purpose of continuing the play.
—James Carse

It's a funny thing
that when a man hasn't anything on earth to worry about,
he goes off and gets married.
—Robert Frost

Golf helps you to understand how you act. Marriage helps you to understand why you act.

Marriage is not a game in the sense that golf is a game. However, marriage can be viewed as a game from the standpoint of trying to understand rules that guide you in doing things that make you feel like you're gaining something.

In golf, you play the infinite game by happily looking for incremental improvements in all the different and subtle phases of the game:

- Ability to instantaneously recognize the state of the relationship between your mind-body system and your golf swing

- Ability to address changes by making adjustments in the amount of time needed to get centered over the ball before starting your swing

- Amount of energy you can generate with your coil-uncoil swing motion

- Efficiency with which that energy is transferred to the ball

- Percentage of club-face sweet spot that impacts the ball

- Ability to control the swing plane and manage yourself around the course

- Understanding the characteristics of the putting surface, etc.

All provide opportunities for playing the infinite game and making your golf game an unending source of pleasure and personal growth regardless of what your score happens to be that day.

Playing the infinite game with your marriage is very similar. The marriage infinite game has you continuously looking for incremental improvements in your ability to be with the relationship when it's stressing you out. Just as there are several phases involved in the development of your golf game, there are many phases involved in the development of your marriage. With marriage, you must learn to be together, act together, dream together, grieve together, play together, pray together, and live together. You must also learn to do all of these things apart in a way that not only supports the growth of the relationship but moves it in the direction of your intent.

Playing the infinite game helps get your mind in the right place to be able to do this.

For example, seek small improvements in your understanding of where your spouse is coming from emotionally, before you pass judgment on what was said or done. Seek incremental improvements in your reflexes and habits, like taking a few deep breaths before responding to what feels like hostile, threatening, or totally confusing input from your partner. Spend a few seconds reminding yourself of your larger intent before deciding what to say or do about the action or statement made by your spouse.

Breaking your actions down into their smallest parts, and taking a critical and self-encouraging look at each part with the aim of continually evolving your appreciation of it, will help you learn to play the infinite game. That, in turn, will just about guarantee you an improved golf experience and greater fulfillment in your marriage. In golf, you will become less inclined to view equipment, conditions, course layout, etc., as enemies and more inclined to view these things as facilitators of that day's lessons. Similarly, in marriage you will begin to see your spouse's perceived failings less as something satanic and more as something you can learn from. You may still have trouble breaking par on a regular basis, and your marriage may not last until death do you part, but chances are that both relationships will be healthier, and it will become easier for you to find ways to keep them both growing.

Playing the infinite game creates more pleasure for you, because you'll realize that as long as you continue to play it, you can't lose. Knowing that you can't lose makes it easy to relax and be present with that good energy. There's no need to check and see whether you're winning or losing, because your emotional closure doesn't come from a score. Rather, it comes from the joy of continuing to play the game. For most, this might be easier to do for golf than marriage, because the style and method you use to deal with frustration in marriage might cause you to unknowingly worsen the problem or set the stage for even greater frustration. If that happens, consider it a part of that day's lesson.

Appreciation for the infinite-game concept will grow as you mature. As you get older, the things you consider victories become smaller (e.g., remembering where you put your car keys or remembering, on the second tee, the names of at least two of three people you met on the first tee).

In the infinite game, the focus is not on winning or losing, but on continuing to play.

Chapter 19

The Rainbow Is the Pot of Gold

Bachelors know more about women than married men;
if they didn't they'd be married too.
—H. L. Mencken

Realize deeply that the present moment is all you ever have.
Make the now the primary focus of your life.
—Eckhart Tolle

In golf and in marriage, getting there is not as important as getting what you can get while getting there.

Throughout their lives, people tend to focus on achieving some singular thing or list of things, working hard to reach that pot of gold at the end of the rainbow. What we must realize is that we create that pot of gold by learning to fully appreciate the rainbow as we go along. Besides, the pot of gold we expect to find at the end of the rainbow may not to be there.

Putting so much focus on the end of the rainbow could well cause us to miss out on all the beauty and wonder of the things we do on our way there. The fabled pot of gold actually equates to the sum total of everything we encounter and all the efforts we make while trying to reach it.

In golf, the pot of gold might be the day you shoot a score under par. Perhaps you're an accomplished player, and your pot of gold is reaching a level that puts you on the professional circuit. Or maybe it comes on that day you break your club's course record. On the other hand, you might be of a more modest mind, someone whose pot of gold comes when you become the lowest handicap in your regular Sunday foursome. Each of these goals (or pots of gold) will require many small successes and developmental experiences—the things that constitute your rainbow.

In marriage, the pot of gold is not so simple or so easily quantified. Maybe you look forward to the day that your wife or husband finally understands you and doesn't give you any more crap when you try to explain something! Or perhaps the marriage pot of gold becomes your reality when your spouse lets you take the lead on all important decisions and you never, ever argue again. Or maybe it's when the two of you finally settle into a long and peaceful retirement together. However you envision your pot of gold, too much focus on what might be out there (timewise) might mean that you're not taking advantage of what's going on right in front of you—that you're missing the wealth, wonder, and other benefits of the rainbow itself. It's like missing the beauty and aroma of the flowers while walking across a field to get from point A to point B. We've already discussed mission clarity and how important that is, but remember that getting the mission accomplished is a function of what you put into each day (the rainbow).

We learn golf one small step at a time. Each instance where you address the ball offers up a complete adventure in itself. You just need to see it as such and be open to taking in that moment. The rainbow comprises that multitude of efforts and realizations that go into developing a single skill associated with your golf swing:

- Recognizing how it feels to be physically, mentally, and emotionally centered over the ball prior to taking the club back

- Learning to be receptive and sensitive to the feedback the golf club gives you when contact is made with the ball, the ground, or both

- Learning to savor that cathartic release as your body converts potential energy into kinetic energy during the uncoiling process

- Recognizing the joy you get from moving toward the ability to instantly center yourself

These are just a few of the many things awaiting your attention as you develop your game—this is your rainbow, which becomes your pot of gold when you recognize and savor it as such. It's the process of achieving incremental growth that gives rise to the ultimate benefit and reward, no matter how fast or slow your growth seems to be.

Marriage offers the same opportunities. Each time you encounter a challenge, decision point, or just a routine decision to be made with your intimate partner, it's like addressing the ball in golf.

When issues crop up during the early stages of marriage, you try to deal with the increase in your heart rate, the anxiety, the tension, the fear-laden anticipation, and the tendency to become defensive—all while expecting the worst. Eventually, you learn to keep yourself centered mentally, physically, and emotionally so you can allow yourself to relate to and even appreciate the benefits that come from dealing with that issue successfully. The result is reduced tension, less anxiety, etc.— thus helping to eliminate things that might otherwise compound the problem.

Embracing the rainbow itself as the pot of gold will help to free you up emotionally. This will aid you and your partner to feel each other's commitment to the relationship.

Funeral

Two elderly gentlemen, Jim and Dave, were midway through their round of golf. As they were about to putt out on the tenth green, a funeral procession drove by. Jim turned to face the procession, stood quietly, and put his hand over his heart.

Dave looked at him and said, "I didn't know you were so sentimental about funerals." Jim replied, "It's the least I can do - we were married for thirty years."

Chapter 20

Good Marriages and Good Golf Feed Each Other

The odds are strong, however,
that most of us have gotten more training in learning how to drive
than in learning how to love.
—Virginia Johnson

Thinking instead of acting is the number-one golf disease.
—Sam Snead

A good marriage grows stronger with time. A good golf swing helps create the time, space, and energy to grow a good marriage.

To borrow a line from Christopher Plummer in a recent movie: "We should concern ourselves not so much with the pursuit of happiness, but with the happiness of pursuit."

In an earlier chapter I spoke about the ability of golf to strip people of their façades. This is great news for both the player and his playing partners. Your partners get to know you better, and you get to know you better. Any endeavor that tends to bring the real you out into the open is one that can play a big role in helping you get the most out of life. Marriage does this by placing you in a situation where you need to deal with two big emotional roller coasters (yours and your partner's) at the same time. Because those roller coasters are operating on different track layouts, total control will be impossible.

Golf does it by placing you in a relationship that will continually remind you how awful you can be at trying to do something that looks like it should be so easy. In both marriage and golf, we see a great opportunity for self-discovery. You can take advantage of that opportunity by holding the attitude that keeps you learning about yourself and working to further develop the way your mental, physical, and emotional parts relate to one another.

Good marriages and good golf happen when time is used mainly in good treks of self-discovery. The best treks of self-discovery come from being willing to open up and connect with those things that seem to bother you most about your relationship.

Since about the middle of the twentieth century there's been a big increase in the number of men and women talking about and embarking upon journeys of self-discovery. Some of the worst of these were chemically induced. But generally speaking people use this phrase to refer to a kind of pilgrimage, an actual physical journey to some distant place. We learn about these seekers in books, magazines, and movies (e.g. *The National Geographic* or *Eat, Pray, Love*) where people go off to some exotic land with a fierce determination to find themselves. Many go on a religiously inspired journey that takes them to some holy site such as Jerusalem or Mecca, where they hope to achieve some form of existential closure or prepare themselves for the afterlife. Others choose even more adventurous excursions - for example, walking across a desert or sailing alone on the high seas.

One of the classic literary treatments of a self-discovery journey can be found in Hermann Hesse's 1922 novel *Siddhartha*. The name Siddhartha can be loosely translated from Sanskrit to mean, appropriately, "he who has found the meaning of existence." In the end, Siddhartha does find enlightenment, by means of what I would call an intense and focused effort to pay attention to the simplest aspects of where he is and what he's doing.

Most who undertake self-discovery journeys, while they may have had a wonderful adventure and learned a lot about life, come to realize that it wasn't really necessary to travel halfway around the world to find themselves. Their true self was right there all along, in the place they've been calling home for most of their lives! But if it takes a big trip to learn that, then so be it.

Sometimes it can seem easier to conquer the Himalayas than to deal with a problem in your marriage. But before you go off on that great journey to the other side of the planet, it might be a good idea to first go back to the bedroom, the dinner table, or the family room and try to figure out what you need to do to climb the emotional mountain that awaits you there.

When an Australian Aborigine heads into the wilderness on a walkabout, he's basically setting out to attempt a reset of his spirit and engage in a rite of passage. The walkabout is a trek of self-discovery and natural education that can last for months. When he completes it successfully (i.e., survives), he has become a wiser and more spiritually energized, mature, and emotionally settled person.

Each time you step onto the golf course is like taking a little walkabout. Call it a golfabout. Not only are you out walking (the worse you play, the more you walk), but at some point you'll probably need to call on your best emotional survival skills. You're likely to find yourself trying to come to grips with fears, insecurities, and frustrations that force you to admit some things to yourself that just might feel a bit embarrassing.

In marriage, there are different types of walkabouts. One is called the talkabout. In that one, you must learn to talk about things you would really prefer to ignore. You must learn to talk about why you are the way you are, even though you may not have the answers or even be comfortable with knowing them. You may need to talk about your spouse's feelings and your own. Now there's an adventure for you!

There are times when your marriage can force you to take a real Aborigine-type walkabout to put some time and distance between you and your spouse. This can free your mind to figure out the next best move for saving the marriage. (Golf courses can be good for this purpose.)

According to Rabbi Aryeh Pamensky, founder of *HappyWife.com*, a good and successful marriage is one where there is "a lifetime commitment to constantly provide emotional intimacy to your spouse, thereby uncovering your true self and, ultimately, your unique purpose for being created."

Let's say we buy that. The question still remains: How do we actually do it?

When we take another look at Rabbi Pamensky's definition, we see that he presents several very big concepts: lifetime commitment, constant emotional intimacy, your true self, your unique purpose for being. Each of these ideas alone is challenging enough to command all the attention and focus the average human being might muster in a lifetime. It seems that what he's really talking about here is using your marriage relationship as a vehicle to help you achieve self-actualization. Or perhaps he's saying that your spiritual evolution is a function of finding another person who's willing to be your emotional proving ground as you develop the skills to battle your own demons. Either way, I believe the good rabbi is on to something with his description, because, depending on your intent, these are the things you'll actually try to do in order to keep your relationship moving forward.

Other views on the attainment of a good and successful marriage are more basic. To keep it simple, some guys like to say, "Happy wife, happy life." That sounds basic enough. Just make her happy and keep her that way, and marriage becomes a piece of cake. The problem with this approach is that you can't make her happy. Conversely, she can't make you happy. One of the biggest traps couples fall into is trying to make their partner accountable for their own happiness. In a good marriage, your spouse becomes a co-discoverer on your journey of self-discovery, but the relationship you have with yourself remains the only long-term source of true happiness. Your golf and marriage relationships give you a vehicle for developing that relationship with yourself.

Conclusion

There are published Twelve-Step recovery programs for victims of abusive golf and marriage relationships. This is not one of them.

Golf and Marriage isn't meant to detox you. Rather, it's about realizing that finding joy (or more joy) in one part of your life can increase satisfaction in other parts.

All the talk of being mindful and studying paths to enlightenment is not meant to suggest that you must become like the Buddha or the Dalai Lama. (The last time I checked, I don't think either of them was married or played golf.) These ideas are presented because injecting them into your routine can actually make you less inclined to call a divorce lawyer (or throw a club) when trouble comes up. Yes, I know the implications of failing at marriage are much greater than those of failing at golf. With golf you can just say, "To hell with it, I'm going back to tennis." In marriage, deciding "To hell with it" could make you the "it."

Try not to think of your marriage or your golf game as being about winning or happiness in the usual sense. Instead, think of them as opportunities to gain a kind of clarity while extending personal boundaries. Success in life doesn't come from being problem-free. It comes from being free to have problems, while knowing that you can put them to work for you.

There are those who believe that the average person can never truly get a handle on either golf or marriage, because both are such seemingly unnatural acts. But if you just keep the fundamentals in mind—**S**elf-knowledge, **A**wareness, **M**anaging expectations, **I**ntent, **A**ttitude and habits, and **M**ission clarity (**SAM-I-AM**)—then with a bit of perseverance, it can be done.

Now when you grab your clubs and head out to the links, you can tell your significant other that you're going out to work on becoming a better partner in life. That should put a smile on his or her face.

Epilogue (not a true story)

Once upon a time in a place called the Garden of Eden, Adam awakened from a deep, restful sleep and found a set of beautiful new golf clubs beside him. Just looking at them, Adam knew such craftsmanship and beauty could only have been fashioned in Heaven.

Adam looked up and almost swallowed his "apple" when he saw the most wonderful links-style golf course, the likes of which he knew only a God could design and build. Thinking, *The Lord is truly all-powerful and all-knowing,* Adam could hardly contain his excitement at the anticipation of getting out on the course. Adam then heard the booming voice of God say, "Adam, you may go forth and enjoy this magnificent links for as long as your heart desires."

Adam rejoiced as he jumped up, grabbed the clubs, and headed out to the number one tee for a heavenly round of buck-naked golf. Before Adam could get very far though, God said, "Adam, there is one condition you must abide by."

"Yes, Lord?" Adam waited.

In that same instant, a thick booklet appeared at Adam's feet, entitled *Rules of Golf.* "See the book at your feet?" said the Lord. "You must strictly obey the rules therein at all times."

Adam picked up the book and pleaded, "But Lord, there are dozens of rules in here, with hundreds of subsections and hundreds more explanatory notes!"

God replied, "as it is written, let it be done."

Adam tried again. "But Lord—" he began, then realized it was no use, as God had turned a deaf ear to his pleading. Adam quickly read the rule book then headed out to the course, looking forward to a golden round of golf.

All was going well as Adam made the turn three under par. When he got to number eleven, it was a devilish-looking par five with a tight dogleg to the right that wrapped around deep fescue and a big water hazard. Adam had been striping the fairways with his driver all day and so was confident that he could cut the corner and position himself for a go at the green in two.

His drive flew straight and true, landing on the right-center of the fairway but taking an unfortunate bounce into the rough. As Adam approached his ball position, he saw that it was just barely in the rough. He stood pondering his next shot when he heard a smooth, enticing voice say, "Hey, it's barely in the rough. Just bump it out with your toe and you'll be in good shape to go for the green—eagle putt. Go ahead, no one will see you kick it out."

Adam looked at his caddy, the serpent, and said: "Are you sure it's okay? Remember what God said." The serpent replied, "Sure it's okay. God just made up those rules so no one would beat his course record. Go ahead, just kick it out a little bit."

So Adam eased the ball a few inches out of the rough with the toe of his right foot, being as quick and inconspicuous as he could. He then pulled his shiny new five-metal from the bag and began his pre-shot routine.

Just as he started his backswing, Adam felt the earth tremble and there was a violent thunderclap. A booming voice demanded, "Adam, why hast thou violated rules thirteen-one and thirteen-two?" Frightened to the point of shaking uncontrollably, Adam finally responded, "Oh, Lord, this is my first time on this course, and I'm not clear on all the local rules, so I asked my caddy, the serpent. He assured me it would be okay, in this instance, to move the ball."

Angrily, God turned to the serpent saying, "For your treachery and defiance, from now and evermore thou shalt crawl, facing the dust of the earth and looking up to all other animals as you are the lowest of the low."

The serpent slithered off into the tall grass, muttering expletives and something about unfairness and insanity. He was not seen or heard of again.

God's attention turned to Adam. "For your misdeed and disobedience," you are hereby banned from Eden for all time. You must go now to the clubhouse and there meet the woman Eve, who will teach you the ways of life."

Adam picked up his clubs and slowly, sadly started to make his way to the clubhouse. He had only taken a few steps when he heard the big voice say, "Stop!"

"Yes, Lord?"

"Leave the clubs!" the voice commanded.

Adam dropped the golf bag and walked on. In front of the clubhouse entrance was a small table with an assortment of fig leaves and a sign that read, "All players must be covered before entering." Adam picked out a fig leaf, covered his nakedness and walked inside.

The clubhouse bar was called the "Land of Nod," and it was there that Adam saw Eve, standing by the exit with her arms folded across her chest. He walked up to her and introduced himself. "Hi! I'm Adam. The Lord told me I was to—"

She interrupted before he could finish. "Yes, I know who you are and I also know you have a lot to learn."

Adam just lowered his head pitifully.

Eve continued. "I will teach you the ways of life - let's go. You can start by taking out the garbage."

About the Author

Garey Johnson grew up in Benton Harbor, Michigan, and received his doctorate from the School of Public Administration at the University of Southern California after studying electrical engineering, quantum physics, international business, and systems management. His doctoral work was nationally recognized and earned him 'Dissertation of the Year' honors from the American Society for Public Administration.

A lifelong serious athlete, Dr. Johnson has played many sports. As a collegiate, he played basketball and football and received tryout invitations from NBA and NFL franchises. A third-degree black belt in Korean karate, he regularly competed in national and international tournaments and garnered the title of Western States Karate Champion. As a captain in the United States Air Force, he was the head martial arts instructor at Williams Air Force Base as well as a senior instructor pilot in supersonic jet aircraft.

Dr. Johnson currently holds a single-digit golf handicap and has played golf in seventeen different countries. His favorite golfing venue is Bandon Dunes Golf Resort in Oregon. He, his wife, and their two teenage children reside in California's San Francisco Bay Area.